Help Me! Guide to the iPhone 5

By Charles Hughes

Table of Contents

Getting Started

Table of Contents

1. Button Layout

The iPhone has four buttons and one switch. The rest of the functionality is controlled by the touchscreen. Each button has several functions, depending on the context in which it is used. The iPhone buttons perform the following functions:

**Sleep/Wake
Button**

Figure 1: Top View

Sleep/Wake Button - Turns the iPhone on and off. Locks and unlocks the iPhone.

Figure 2: Front View

Home Button - Shows the Home screen. Displays open applications when pressed twice quickly.

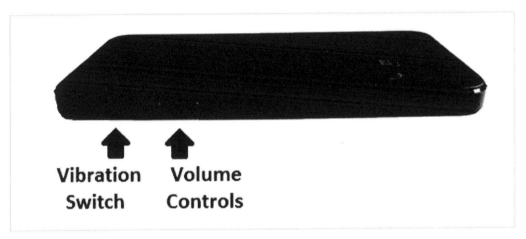

Figure 3: Side View

Volume Controls - Control the volume of the ringer. Refer to *"Adjusting the Settings"* on page 205 to learn more about setting ringtones or the sound volume. Control the volume of the earpiece or speakerphone during a conversation. Control the media volume.

Vibration Switch - Turns Silent mode on or off. The iPhone will vibrate in Silent mode if vibration is turned on.

Figure 4: Bottom View

Headphone Jack - Allows headphones or speakers to be plugged in. Allows an AUX cable to be plugged in to hear the iPhone over the speakers in a car or stereo.

Lightning Connector - Connects the iPhone to a computer in order to transfer data. Connects the iPhone to a charger.

2. Charging the iPhone

To ensure that the iPhone works well, please follow these guidelines:

Note: You cannot use a cable that came with any earlier generation iPhone to charge the iPhone 5.

Discharge the iPhone completely at least once a month. When charging the battery, the meter in the upper right-hand corner of the screen (when unlocked) may show that it is fully charged; however, the charge is not complete until the battery icon looks like this: ▬ While the iPhone is charging, the icon will look like this: ▬ . Insert the Lightning cable into the Lightning Connector on the bottom of the phone. When the cable is inserted correctly, the indicator sound is played or the iPhone vibrates. The wallpaper is also changed to a picture of a battery, as shown in **Figure 5**. Note that the wallpaper changes to show the battery charge. Refer to *"Tips and Tricks"* on page 285 to learn about conserving battery life.

Figure 5: Charging Wallpaper

3. Turning the iPhone On and Off

Use the Sleep/Wake button to turn the iPhone on or off. To turn the iPhone on, press and hold the

Sleep/Wake button for two seconds. The iPhone turns on and the 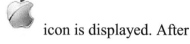 icon is displayed. After the iPhone has finished starting up, the Lock screen is displayed.

Note: If the iPhone does not turn on after a few seconds, try charging the battery.

To turn the iPhone off, press and hold the Sleep/Wake button until the screen becomes dark. The message "Slide to power off" appears. Touch the ➡ slider and move your finger to the right. The iPhone turns off.

Note: To keep the iPhone on, press "Cancel" or do not take any action at all.

4. Installing a SIM Card

Insert the SIM card from an old phone to retain your personal information. To install a SIM card:

1. Turn off the iPhone. Refer to *"Turning the iPhone On and Off"* on page 16 to learn how.
2. Insert the end of a paper clip or a SIM eject tool into the hole on the right side of the iPhone. The SIM card tray pops out.
3. Take out the old SIM card, if necessary, and insert the new SIM card with the short side facing upwards.
4. Re-insert the tray into the iPhone. The new SIM card is installed.

5. Setting Up the iPhone for the First Time

You must set up the iPhone 5 when you turn it on for the first time. To set up the iPhone 5:

1. Turn on the iPhone by pressing and holding the Power button until the icon appears. The iPhone starts up and the Welcome screen appears, as shown in **Figure 6**.

2. Touch the ➡ slider and move it to the right to begin setting up your iPhone. The Language screen appears, as shown in **Figure 7**.

3. Touch the preferred language. If you need to view more languages, touch the 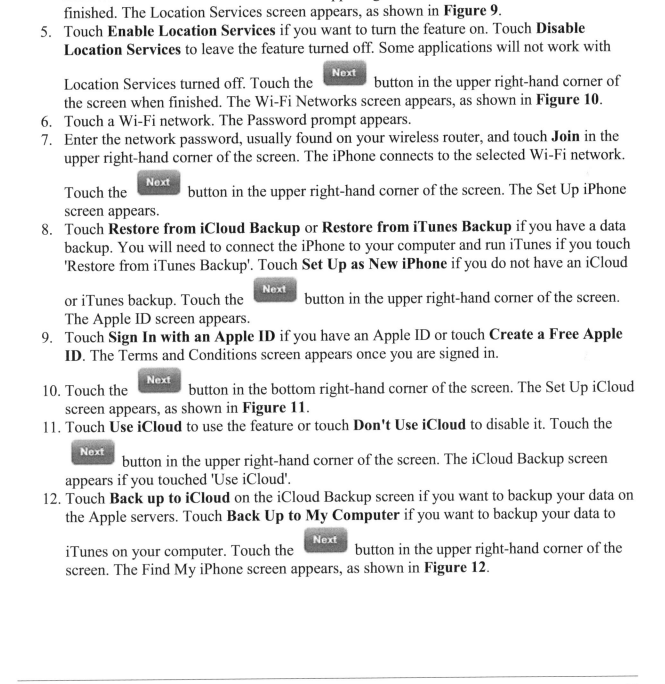 and then touch the desired language. Touch the button in the upper right-hand corner of the screen when finished. The language is selected and the Country screen appears, as shown in **Figure 8**.

4. Touch the country in which you reside. If you need to view more countries, touch Show More... Touch the **Next** button in the upper right-hand corner of the screen when finished. The Location Services screen appears, as shown in **Figure 9**.

5. Touch **Enable Location Services** if you want to turn the feature on. Touch **Disable Location Services** to leave the feature turned off. Some applications will not work with Location Services turned off. Touch the **Next** button in the upper right-hand corner of the screen when finished. The Wi-Fi Networks screen appears, as shown in **Figure 10**.

6. Touch a Wi-Fi network. The Password prompt appears.

7. Enter the network password, usually found on your wireless router, and touch **Join** in the upper right-hand corner of the screen. The iPhone connects to the selected Wi-Fi network. Touch the **Next** button in the upper right-hand corner of the screen. The Set Up iPhone screen appears.

8. Touch **Restore from iCloud Backup** or **Restore from iTunes Backup** if you have a data backup. You will need to connect the iPhone to your computer and run iTunes if you touch 'Restore from iTunes Backup'. Touch **Set Up as New iPhone** if you do not have an iCloud or iTunes backup. Touch the **Next** button in the upper right-hand corner of the screen. The Apple ID screen appears.

9. Touch **Sign In with an Apple ID** if you have an Apple ID or touch **Create a Free Apple ID**. The Terms and Conditions screen appears once you are signed in.

10. Touch the **Next** button in the bottom right-hand corner of the screen. The Set Up iCloud screen appears, as shown in **Figure 11**.

11. Touch **Use iCloud** to use the feature or touch **Don't Use iCloud** to disable it. Touch the **Next** button in the upper right-hand corner of the screen. The iCloud Backup screen appears if you touched 'Use iCloud'.

12. Touch **Back up to iCloud** on the iCloud Backup screen if you want to backup your data on the Apple servers. Touch **Back Up to My Computer** if you want to backup your data to iTunes on your computer. Touch the **Next** button in the upper right-hand corner of the screen. The Find My iPhone screen appears, as shown in **Figure 12**.

Figure 6: Welcome Screen

Figure 7: Language Screen

Figure 8: Country Screen

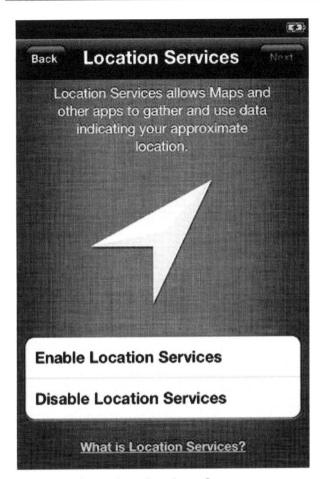

Figure 9: Location Services Screen

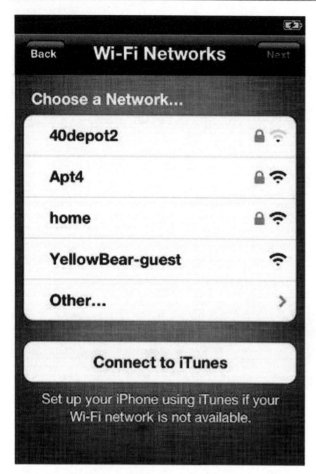

Figure 10: Wi-Fi Networks Screen

Figure 11: Set Up iCloud Screen

Figure 12: Find My iPhone Screen

6. Navigating the Screens

There are many ways to navigate the iPhone. Use the following tips to quickly navigate the screens of the iPhone:

- Use the Home button to return to the Home screen at any time. Any application or tool that you were using will be in the same state when you return to it.
- At the Home screen, slide your finger to the left to access additional screens. If nothing happens, the other screens are blank.
- At the Home screen, slide your finger to the right to access the iPhone's search feature. On this page, you may search any data stored on your phone, including application data.
- Use the [   ] button at the top left of most menus to return to the previous screen. For instance, when adjusting the Sound settings, touch the [Settings] button to go back to the Settings Screen, as outlined in **Figure 13**.

Figure 13: Sound Settings Menu

7. Organizing Icons

You may wish to re-order the location of the application icons on the screens. To organize application icons:

1. Touch an icon and hold it until all of the icons begin to shake. The icons can now be moved around the screen.
2. Move the icon to the desired location and let go of the screen. The icon is relocated and the surrounding icons are re-ordered accordingly. If an icon that used to be on the screen is gone, then it has been moved to a different Home screen in the process.
3. To move an icon to another screen, move the icon to the edge of the current one and hold it there. The adjacent screen appears. Drop the icon in the desired location.
4. Press the **Home** button. The icons stop shaking.

8. Creating an Icon Folder

When there are many icons on the Home screens, you may wish to organize the icons into folders. Each folder can have a meaningful name to enable you to find the icons easily. To create a folder:

1. Touch an icon and hold it until all of the icons begin to shake. The icons can now be moved.
2. Move one icon on top of another and let go of the screen. A folder with those two icons is created, as shown in **Figure 14**. Touch the ⊗ button to enter a name for the folder.
3. Enter a name for the folder and touch the [Done] button. The new name is saved.
4. To exit the folder, touch anywhere outside of it. The folder closes.
5. Press the **Home** button. The icons stop shaking.

Note: To add more icons to a folder, just touch an icon while it is shaking and move it onto the folder.

Figure 14: A New Folder on the iPhone

9. Using Wi-Fi

Use a nearby Wi-Fi hotspot or a home router to attain a much faster internet connection than 4G. Wi-Fi is required to download large applications and to use FaceTime. To turn on Wi-Fi:

1. Touch the ![settings icon] icon. The Settings screen appears.
2. Touch **Wi-Fi**. The Wi-Fi Networks screen appears.
3. Touch the ![OFF switch] switch next to 'Wi-Fi'. Wi-Fi turns on and a list of available networks appears, as shown in **Figure 15**. If the network has an ![lock icon] icon next to it, a password is needed to connect to it.
4. Touch the network to which you would like to connect. The Password screen appears if the network is protected.
5. Enter the network password. Touch **Join** in the bottom right-hand corner of the screen. Provided that you entered the correct password, a check mark appears next to the network name and the ![wifi icon] icon appears at the top of the screen, as shown in **Figure 16**. You are connected to the Wi-Fi network.

Note: If you enter an incorrect password, the message "Incorrect password for >Network Name<" appears, where '>Network Name<' is the name of your network. The network password is usually written on the modem given to you by your internet service provider. It is sometimes called a WEP Key.

Figure 15: Available Wi-Fi Network List

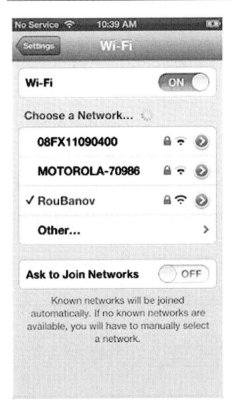

Figure 16: Wi-Fi Connected

Making Voice and Video Calls

Table of Contents

1. Dialing a Number

Numbers that are not in your Phonebook can be dialed on the keypad. To manually dial a phone number:

1. Touch the ![icon] icon on the Home screen. The Phonebook appears.
2. Touch the ![icon] icon at the bottom of the screen. The Keypad appears, as shown in **Figure 1**.
3. Enter the desired phone number and then touch the ![Call button] button at the bottom of the screen. The iPhone dials the number.

Note: If an incorrect number is entered, "Error Performing Request - Unknown Error" appears.

Figure 1: Keypad

2. Calling a Contact

If a number is stored in your Phonebook, you may touch the name of a contact to dial it. To call a contact already stored in your iPhone:

1. Touch the ![icon] icon on the Home screen. The Contacts screen appears.
2. Touch the name of the desired contact. The Contact Information screen appears, as shown in **Figure 2**.
3. Touch the desired phone number. The iPhone calls the contact's number. Refer to *"Managing Contacts"* on page 50 to learn more about adding or removing contacts.

Figure 2: Contact Information Screen

3. Calling a Favorite

There is no Speed Dial feature on the iPhone. Instead, frequently dialed numbers can be saved as Favorites, which can be accessed more quickly. To call a number stored in Favorites:

1. Touch the 📞 icon on the Home screen. The Calling screen appears.
2. Touch the ⭐ icon at the bottom of the screen. The Favorites screen appears, as shown in **Figure 3**.
3. Touch the name of a Favorite. The iPhone calls the selected number. Refer to *"Managing Contacts"* on page 50 to learn more about managing Favorites.

Figure 3: Favorites Screen

4. Returning a Recent Phone Call

After missing a call, your iPhone will notify you of who called and at what time. The iPhone also shows a history of all recently placed calls. To view and return a missed call or redial a recently entered number:

1. Touch the ![icon] icon on the Home screen. The Calling screen appears.
2. Touch the ![icon] icon at the bottom of the screen. The Recent Calls screen appears, with the most recent calls on top. Missed or declined calls are shown in red. The ![icon] icon is shown next to a placed call, as outlined in **Figure 4**.
3. Touch the name of a contact. The iPhone dials the contact.

Note: To view only missed calls, touch the *button at the top of the recent calls screen.*

Figure 4: Recent Calls Screen

5. Receiving a Voice Call

There are several ways to accept or reject a voice call based on whether or not the screen is locked. Use the following tips when receiving a voice call:

- To receive an incoming voice call while the iPhone is locked, touch and move the on the slider, shown in **Figure 5**, to the right. The call is answered.
- To mute the ringer, press the **Sleep/Wake** button. To reject the incoming call, press the **Sleep/Wake** button again.
- To receive an incoming call while using an application (or viewing a Home screen), touch the button, as shown in **Figure 6**. To reject the incoming call, touch the

  button. The call is declined. The number then shows up in red in the list of

  recent calls, signifying that it is a missed call, and a notification appears above the

  icon on the Home screen.

- Touch the icon and slide it up to bring up two additional options: 'Reply with Message' and 'Remind Me Later'. Refer to *"Replying to an Incoming Call with a Text Message"* on page 41 or *"Setting a Reminder to Return an Incoming Call"* on page 42 to learn more about these options.

Figure 5: Incoming Call, iPhone Locked

Figure 6: Incoming Call, iPhone Unlocked

6. Replying to an Incoming Call with a Text Message

During an incoming call, you may reject it and automatically send a text message to the caller. To reply to an incoming call with a text message:

1. Touch the ▬ icon and slide it up during an incoming voice call. The Call Reject options appear at the bottom of the screen, as shown in **Figure 7**.
2. Touch **Reply with Message**. A list of pre-defined text messages appear.
3. Touch a message. The selected text message is sent to the caller. Alternatively, touch **Custom** to enter your own text message.
4. Touch the **Send** button. The iPhone sends the custom text message to the caller.

Figure 7: Call Reject Options

7. Setting a Reminder to Return an Incoming Call

During an incoming call, you may reject it and automatically set a reminder for yourself to return the call at a specified time or when you reach a specific location (such as work or home). To set a reminder to return an incoming call:

1. Touch the [icon] icon and slide it up during an incoming voice call. The Call Reject options appear at the bottom of the screen.
2. Touch **Remind Me Later**. The following reminder options appear: 'In 1 hour' and 'When I leave'.
3. Touch **In 1 hour**. The iPhone displays a pop-up after one hour has passed reminding you to call back. Alternatively, touch **When I leave** to have the iPhone remind you when you leave your current location.

8. Using the Speakerphone During a Voice Call

The iPhone has a built-in Speakerphone, which is useful when calling from a car or when several people need to hear the conversation. To use the Speakerphone during a phone call:

1. Place a voice call. The Calling Screen appears, as shown in **Figure 8**.

2. Touch the [icon] icon. The Speakerphone is turned on. Adjust the volume of the Speakerphone by using the Volume Controls. Refer to *"Button Layout"* on page 11 to locate the Volume Controls.

3. Touch the [icon] icon. The Speakerphone is turned off.

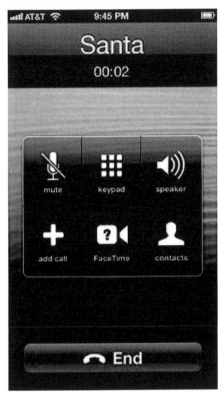

Figure 8: Calling Screen

9. Using the Keypad During a Voice Call

You may wish to use the keypad while on a call in orer to input numbers in an automated menu or to enter an account number. To use the keypad during a phone call, place a voice call and touch the icon. The keypad appears. To hide the keypad again, touch **Hide Keypad**.

10. Using the Mute Function During a Voice Call

During a voice call, you may wish to mute your side of the conversation. When mute is turned on, the person on the other end of the line will not hear anything on your side. To use Mute during a

call, place a voice call and touch the icon. The iPhone mutes your voice and the caller(s)

can no longer hear you, but you are still able to hear them. Touch the icon. Mute is turned off.

11. Putting a Caller on Hold (hidden button)

Apple replaced the Hold button (⏸) with the ？ button on the iPhone 4 and later generations.

However, the Hold function still exists. Press and hold the button while on a call until the ⏸ button appears. Release the screen. The call is put on hold.

12. Starting a Conference Call (Adding a Call)

To talk to more than one person at a time, call another person while continuing the current call. To create a conference call, place a voice call and then touch the ➕ icon. The list of contacts or the keypad is shown. Dial a number or select a contact to call. The first contact is put on hold while the iPhone dials and connects to the second. Touch the ⤋ icon. A three-way conference call is created, as shown in **Figure 9**.

Note: Up to six lines may be included in a conference call.

Figure 9: Three-Way Conference Call

13. Starting a Facetime Call

The iPhone 5 has the ability to place a video call to another iPhone (generation 4 or later), iPad, Mac, or iPod (third generation and on). Facetime on the iPhone 5 does not require a Wi-Fi connection, and you can place and receive calls using a 4G connection (provided that you have at least one bar of service). However, using Wi-Fi may still provide a better video calling experience. Refer to *"Using Wi-Fi"* on page 29 to learn how to turn it on. To place a Facetime call:

1. Touch the icon on the Home screen. The Phonebook appears
2. Touch the name of a contact. The Contact Info screen appears.
3. Touch **Facetime**. A Facetime call is placed. A high-pitched beeping sound plays until the call connects.

4. Touch the button at any time to switch cameras, as outlined in **Figure 10**. Using this feature, you can either show your contact what you are seeing or show them your face. The iPhone 5 can also receive FaceTime calls. To receive an incoming FaceTime call,

   touch the button, as outlined in white in **Figure 11**.

Note: Calling a device that is not compatible with FaceTime or calling a contact that is currently unavailable will result in an error, as shown in **Figure 12**.

Figure 10: Switch Camera Icon

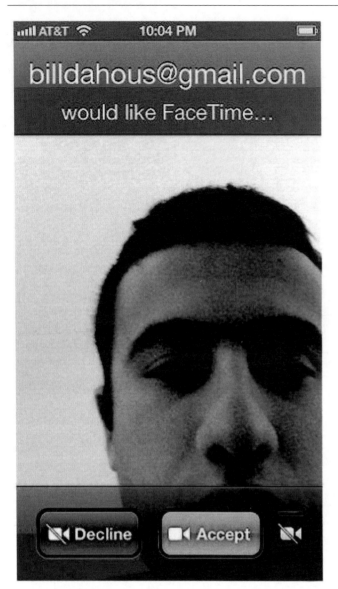

Figure 11: Receiving a FaceTime Call

Figure 12: FaceTime Call Error

Managing Contacts

Table of Contents

1. Adding a New Contact

The iPhone can store phone numbers, email addresses, and other Contact Information in its Phonebook. To add a new contact to the Phonebook:

1. Touch the ![icon] icon on the Home screen. The Phonebook appears, displaying a list of your existing contacts. If a list of all contacts does not appear, touch the **All Contacts** button to view the list.

2. Touch the ![+ button] button in the upper right-hand corner of the screen. The New Contact screen appears, as shown in **Figure 1**.

3. Touch **First**. The keyboard appears. Type the first name of the contact.

4. Touch **Last**. Type the last name of the contact.

5. Touch **Phone**. The keypad appears. Type the contact's phone number. The number is entered.

6. Touch any empty field to enter the desired information, and then touch the **Done** button in the upper right-hand corner of the screen. The contact's information is stored.

Note: Refer to "Tips and Tricks" on page 285 to learn how to add an extension after the contact's phone number.

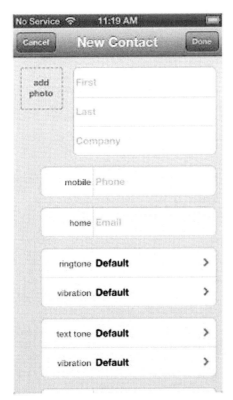

Figure 1: New Contact Screen

2. Finding a Contact

After adding contacts to your iPhone's Phonebook, you may search for them. To find a stored contact:

1. Touch the ![icon] icon on the Home screen. The Phonebook appears. If a list of all contacts does not appear, touch the **All Contacts** button to view the list.
2. Touch **Search**. The keyboard appears.
3. Start typing the name of a contact. Contact matches appear as you type, as shown in **Figure 2**.
4. Touch a match. The Contact Info screen appears, as shown in **Figure 3**.

Figure 2: Contact Matches

Figure 3: Contact Info Screen

3. Deleting a Contact

You may delete contact information from your Phonebook in order to free up space or for organizational purposes. To delete unwanted contact information: Warning: There is no way to restore contact information after it has been deleted.

1. Touch the icon on the Home screen. The Phonebook appears. If a list of all contacts does not appear, touch the **All Contacts** button to view the list.
2. Find and touch the name of the contact you wish to delete. The Contact Info screen appears. Refer to *"Finding a Contact"* on page 52 to learn how.
3. Touch the **Edit** button in the upper right-hand corner of the screen. The Contact Information Editing screen appears.
4. Scroll down and touch the **Delete Contact** button at the bottom of the screen, as outlined in **Figure 4**. A Confirmation menu appears.
5. Touch the **Delete Contact** button again. The contact's information is deleted and will no longer appear in your Phonebook.

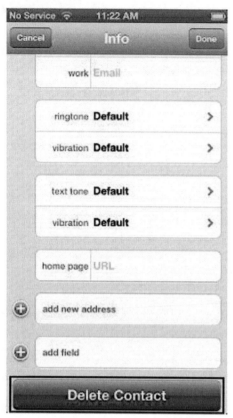

Figure 4: Delete Contact Button Outlined

4. Editing Contact Information

After adding contacts to your Phonebook, you may edit them at any time. To edit an existing contact's information:

1. Touch the ![icon] icon on the Home screen. The Phonebook appears. If a list of all contacts does not appear, touch the **All Contacts** button to view the list.
2. Find and touch a contact's name. The Contact Info screen appears. Refer to *"Finding a Contact"* on page 52 to learn how.
3. Touch the **Edit** button in the upper right-hand corner of the screen. The Contact Editing screen appears.
4. Touch a field to edit the corresponding information. Touch the **Done** button in the upper right-hand corner of the screen. The contact's information is updated.

5. Sharing a Contact's Information

To share a contact's information with someone else:

1. Touch the 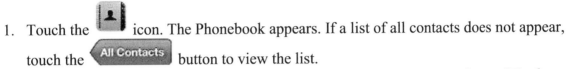 icon. The Phonebook appears. If a list of all contacts does not appear, touch the **All Contacts** button to view the list.
2. Find and touch a contact's name. The Contact Info screen appears. Refer to *"Finding a Contact"* on page 52 to learn how.
3. Touch **Share Contact** in the lower left-hand corner of the screen. The Sharing Options menu appears at the bottom of the screen, as shown in **Figure 5**.
4. Follow the steps in the appropriate section on the following page to email or text the contact's information.

To send the contact's information via email:

1. Touch the **Email** button at the top of the Sharing Options menu. The New Email screen appears, as shown in **Figure 6**. Choose one of the following options for entering the email address:
   - Start typing the name of the contact with whom you wish to share the information. The matching contacts appear. Touch the contact's name. The contact's email address is added.
   - Type the email address from scratch. To use a number, touch **123** at the bottom left of the screen. When done, touch the **return** button in the lower right-hand corner of the screen. Enter more addresses if needed.
   - Touch the ⊕ icon to select as many contacts from your Phonebook or enter as many email addresses as you wish.
2. Enter an optional subject by touching Subject, and touch CC to add other addresses to which to send the information.
3. Touch the **Send** button in the upper right-hand corner of the screen. The contact's information is sent to the selected email addresses. To send a contact's information via multimedia message, touch the **Message** button in the Sharing Options menu. The New Message screen appears, as shown in **Figure 7**. Enter a phone number or phone numbers and touch the **Send** button. The contact's information is sent. There are three methods for entering the phone number:

- Type the phone number from scratch. To use numbers, touch the **123** button at the bottom left of the screen. When done, touch the **return** button in the lower right-hand corner of the screen.

- Touch the ⊕ icon to select one or more contacts from the Phonebook.

Figure 5: Sharing Options Menu

Figure 6: New Message Screen

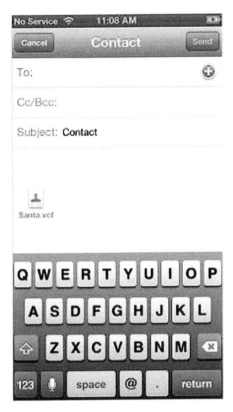

Figure 7: New Email Screen

6. Adding a Contact to Favorites (Speed Dial)

The iPhone has no Speed Dial feature, but the most frequently dialed numbers can be stored as Favorites, which can be accessed more quickly. To add a contact to Favorites:

1. Touch the ![icon] icon on the Home screen. The Phonebook appears. If a list of all contacts does not appear, touch the **All Contacts** button to view the list.
2. Find and touch the contact's name. The Contact Info screen appears. Refer to *"Finding a Contact"* on page 52 to learn search for a contact.
3. Touch **Add to Favorites** in the bottom right-hand corner of the screen. If more than one number is stored for the contact, a menu appears at the bottom of the screen asking you which number should be added. You may also receive a prompt asking you whether the phone should dial the phone number or place a FaceTime called when the favorite is selected.
4. Select the desired number, if applicable, and select the phone or FaceTime number. The contact is added to Favorites. Refer to *"Viewing Favorite Contacts"* on page 62 to learn how to view Favorites.

Note: If there is more than one number stored for a contact, the available numbers appear after touching 'Add Favorites'. Touch the desired number. The number is added to your Favorites.

7. Viewing Favorite Contacts

After adding contacts to Favorites, you may view them at any time. To view your Favorites:

1. Touch the ![icon] icon on the Home screen. The Calling screen that was opened most recently appears.
2. Touch the ![star icon] icon at the bottom left of the screen. The Favorites screen appears, as shown in **Figure 8**. Beside the name of each Favorite is the type of number (i.e. home, mobile, etc.) written in gray letters.
3. Touch the name of a Favorite contact. The iPhone calls the number.

Figure 8: Favorites Screen

8. Removing a Favorite Contact from the List

You may delete a Favorite contact to free up space in your Favorites list. To delete an unwanted Favorite:

1. Open the Favorites screen. Refer to *"Viewing Favorite Contacts"* on page 62 to learn how.
2. Touch the **Edit** button in the upper left-hand corner of the screen. A ⊖ button appears to the left of each favorite contact.
3. Touch the ⊖ button next to the Favorite contact that you wish to delete. The **Delete** button appears to the right of the corresponding name, as outlined in **Figure 9**.
4. Touch the **Delete** button. The Favorite contact is erased. The contact is not deleted from the phonebook.

Note: Touch and hold the ≡ *icon to the right of a Favorite's name to move it. Drag the Favorite to the desired location in the list.*

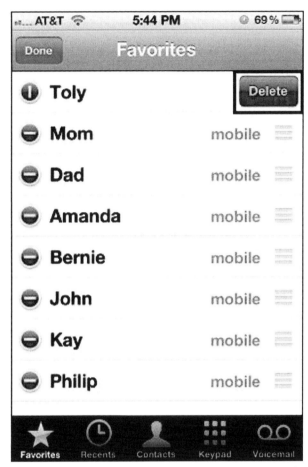

Figure 9: Delete Button on the Favorites Screen

9. Changing the Contact Sort Order

By default, the iPhone sorts the contacts in the Phonebook by last name. For instance, if the names Jane Doe and John Johnson are in the list, John Johnson would come after Jane Doe because 'J' comes after 'D' in the English alphabet. To change the sort order:

1. Touch the  icon. The Settings screen appears, as shown in **Figure 10**.
2. Scroll down and touch **Mail, Contacts, Calendars**. The Mail, Contacts, Calendars screen appears, as shown in **Figure 11**.
3. Scroll down and touch **Sort Order** at the bottom of the screen. The Sort Order screen appears, as shown in **Figure 12**.
4. Touch **First, Last**. A check mark appears to the right of the option and the contacts will be sorted by first name.
5. Touch **Last, First**. A check mark appears to the right of the option and the contacts will be sorted by last name.

Figure 10: Settings Screen

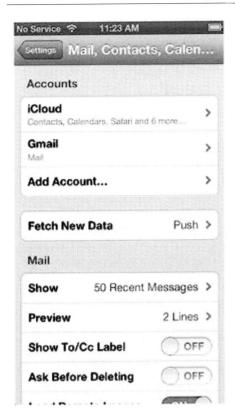

Figure 11: Mail, Contacts, Calendars Screen

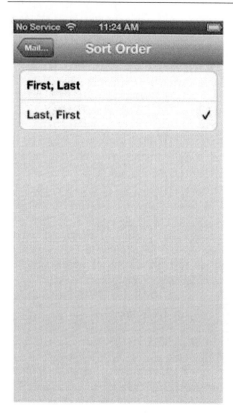

Figure 12: Sort Order Screen

Text Messaging

Table of Contents

1. Composing a New Text Message

The iPhone can send text messages to other mobile phones. To compose a new message:

1. Touch the icon on the Home screen. The Messages screen appears, as shown in **Figure 1**.
2. Touch the button in the upper right-hand corner of the screen. The New Message screen appears, as shown in **Figure 2**.
3. Type the phone number of the recipient. There are three options for entering this information:
   - Start typing the name of the contact. Matching contacts appear as you type. Touch the contact's name. The contact's number is added.
   - Type the phone number from scratch. Touch the button at the bottom left of the screen to enter numbers. When done, touch the button in the lower right-hand corner of the screen. The number is added.
   - Touch the button to select a contact from the Phonebook. Add as many numbers as desired.

4. Touch the text field. The cursor starts flashing at the beginning of the field.
5. Type your message. If you begin to type a word incorrectly, the iPhone may give you a suggestion. To accept the suggestion, touch **Space**. To reject it, touch the ⊗ key to the right of the suggestion.
6. Touch the Send button when finished entering the message. The message is sent. The iPhone shows the progress of the message at the top of the screen. When it is finished sending, a sound is played or the phone vibrates. Your message is shown in a green bubble on the right side of the screen, as shown in **Figure 3**.

All text messages are shown in conversation view. To send a new message to someone you have already texted:

1. Touch the ⬜ icon on the Home screen. The Messages screen appears.
2. Touch the name or number of the recipient. The Conversation screen appears. If the name is not in the list, try scrolling down by touching the screen and moving your finger up. If you cannot find the name, you may have deleted your conversation with that contact.
3. Touch the text field. The cursor starts flashing and a keyboard is shown.
4. Type the message and then touch the Send button. The message is sent. The most recent message that you sent is shown in a green bubble at the bottom right of the conversation. Touch the screen and move your finger down to scroll through older messages.

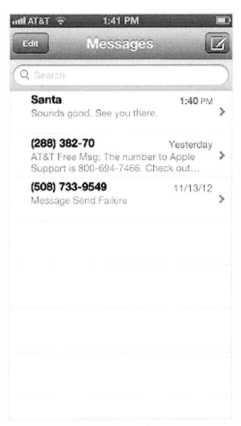

Figure 1: Messages Screen

Figure 2: New Message Screen

Figure 3: Your Message in a Green Bubble

2. Copying, Cutting, and Pasting Text

The iPhone allows you to copy or cut text from one location and paste it to another. Copying leaves the text in its current location and allows you to paste it elsewhere. Cutting deletes the text from its current location and allows you to paste it elsewhere. To cut, copy, and paste text:

1. Touch text in a text field or in a conversation. The Select menu appears above the text, as shown in **Figure 4**. Refer to *"Composing a New Text Message"* on page 69 to learn how to compose a text.
2. Touch **Select All**. All of the text is selected. To select a single word, touch **Select**. Blue dots appear around the word or phrase.
3. Touch and hold one of the blue dots and drag it in any direction. The text between the dots is highlighted and a text menu appears, as shown in **Figure 5**.
4. Touch **Cut** or **Copy**. The corresponding action is taken and the text is ready to be pasted.
5. Touch any empty text field and touch Paste. The text is inserted.

Note: Refer to "Tips and Tricks" on page 285 to learn more about editing text.

Figure 4: Select Menu

Figure 5: Text Menu

3. Using the Spell Check Feature

The iPhone will underline words that are spelled incorrectly with a red dotted line. Touch the underlined word once to see spelling suggestions. Touch a suggestion to substitute the word immediately. If auto-correction is enabled, the iPhone will automatically replace common typos. Over time, the iPhone will learn your most commonly entered words, even names and slang. Refer to *"Adjusting Language and Keyboard Settings"* on page 221 to learn more about auto-correction.

4. Receiving a Text Message

The iPhone can receive text messages from any other mobile device. When the iPhone receives a text, the phone vibrates once or plays a sound, depending on the settings. The New Message notification appears on the Home screen, as shown in **Figure 6**, on the lock screen, as shown in **Figure 7**, or in the Notification Bar at the top of the screen, as outlined in **Figure 8**. Whether the notification appears in the Notification Bar or on the Home screen depends on your settings. Use the following tips when receiving text messages:

- Slide the ⬜ icon to the right on the Lock screen to open the text message.
- Slide the Notification Bar down while running an application. The Notification Center appears, as shown in **Figure 9**. Touch the text message to view it.

- The ① icon next to the ⬜ icon on the Home screen indicates that there is one unread message. This number changes depending on the number of unread messages. The number in the red circle will not disappear until the message is read. Touch the ⬜ icon to view the message.
- Touch **Reply** to send a text back to the contact. The Conversation screen appears.
- Touch **Close** to reply later.

Note: Refer to "Composing a New Text Message" *on page 69 to learn more about sending text messages.*

Figure 6: New Message Notification on the Home Screen

Figure 7: New Message Notification on the Lock Screen

Figure 8: New Message Notification in the Notification Bar

Figure 9: Notification Center

5. Reading a Stored Text Message

You may read any text messages that you have received, provided that you have not deleted them. To read stored text messages:

1. Touch the icon on the Home screen. The Messages screen appears. The iPhone organizes conversations based on the date the last message in the conversation was sent or received, with the most recent conversation at the top of the list.
2. Touch the name of a contact to view the conversation. The Conversation screen appears.
3. Touch the screen and move your finger up and down to scroll through the conversation. The most recent messages appear at the bottom.
4. Touch **Messages** in the upper left-hand corner of the screen. The Messages screen appears.

6. Forwarding a Text Message

You may wish to forward a text message. To forward a text message:

1. Touch the [icon] icon on the Home screen. The Messages screen appears, displaying each sender's name on the left and the date of the message on the right.
2. Touch the conversation that contains the message(s) you wish to forward. The Conversation screen appears.
3. Touch the **Edit** button in the upper right-hand corner of the screen. A gray circle appears to the left of each individual message.
4. Touch the message(s) to forward. Every time a message is selected, a red check mark appears in the gray circle, as shown in **Figure 10**. The parentheses on the **Forward** button show the number of messages selected.
5. Touch the **Forward** button at the bottom of the screen. The New Message screen appears with the selected messages already entered.
6. Start typing the name of a contact or touch the [+] icon to select a number from the Phonebook. The contact is added to the Addressee list.
7. Touch the **Send** button. The message is forwarded to the contacts in the Addressee list.

Figure 10: Selected Messages

7. Calling the Sender from within a Text

After receiving a text message from a contact, you may call that person without ever exiting the text message. To call someone from whom you have received a text message:

1. Touch the  icon on the Home screen. The Messages screen appears. The iPhone organizes conversations based on the date the last message in the conversation was sent or received, with the most recent conversation at the top of the list.
2. Touch the conversation that contains the message(s) from the sender you wish to call. The Conversation screen appears.
3. Touch the top of the screen (where the time and signal icon are displayed). The iPhone scrolls to the top of the conversation.
4. Touch **Call** at the top of the screen. The iPhone places the call.

8. Viewing Sender Information from within a Text

If you have stored a contact's information in the Phonebook, you may view it at any time without leaving a text conversation between the two of you. To view the information of a contact who sent you a message:

1. Touch the icon on the Home screen. The Messages screen appears. The iPhone organizes conversations based on the date the last message in the conversation was sent or received, with the most recent conversation at the top of the list.
2. Touch a conversation. The Conversation screen appears.
3. Touch the screen and move your finger down until the top of the conversation appears.
4. Touch **Contact** in the upper left-hand corner of the screen. The contact's information is displayed.
5. Touch the contact's name in the upper left-hand corner of the screen, as outlined in **Figure 11**. The iPhone returns to the conversation.

Figure 11: Contact Information Screen

9. Deleting a Text Message

The iPhone can delete separate text messages or an entire conversation, which is a series of text messages between you and a contact.

Warning: Once deleted, text messages cannot be restored.

To delete an entire conversation:

1. Touch the ⬤ icon on the Home screen. The Messages screen appears. The iPhone organizes conversations based on the date the last message in the conversation was sent or received, with the most recent conversation at the top of the list.
2. Touch the **Edit** button in the upper left-hand corner of the screen. A ⊖ button appears to the left of each name, as shown in **Figure 12**. If 'Messages' is shown at the top left of the screen, touch **Messages** to return to the Messages screen first, and then touch the **Edit** button.
3. Touch the ⊖ button next to a conversation. The **Delete** button appears next to the contact's name on the right side of the screen.
4. Touch the **Delete** button. The entire conversation is deleted.

To delete a separate text message:

1. Touch the ⬤ icon on the Home screen. The Messages screen appears.
2. Touch a conversation. The conversation screen appears.
3. Touch the **Edit** button in the upper right-hand corner of the screen. A gray circle appears to the left of each individual message.
4. Touch as many separate messages as desired. A red check mark appears in the circle next to each message that you select. The number in parentheses on the **Delete** button at the bottom of the screen indicates the number of messages selected for deletion.
5. Touch the **Delete** button at the bottom of the screen. The selected messages are deleted.

Figure 12: Delete Buttons

10. Sending a Picture Message

You may attach a picture to any text message you send. To send a picture message:

1. Touch the ⬭ icon on the Home screen. The Messages screen appears.

2. Touch the ▣ icon. The New Message screen appears.

3. Touch the ◉ button to the left of the text field. The Photo Attachment menu appears as shown in **Figure 15**. Follow the steps in one of the sections below to either attach an existing picture or take a picture to send:

To attach an existing picture to the text message:

1. Touch the **Choose Existing** button. A list of Photo Albums appears, as shown in **Figure 16**.
2. Touch a photo. The preview of the photo appears.
3. Touch **Choose**. The photo is attached to the text message.

To take a picture and attach it to the text message:

1. Touch the **Take Photo or Video** button. The camera turns on, as shown in **Figure 17**.

2. Touch the ◉ button at the bottom of the screen. The photo is captured and a preview of the photo appears.
3. Touch **Use** to use the photo in the message or touch **Retake** to discard the picture and take another one. The photo is attached.
4. Touch the **Send** button. The picture message is sent.

Note: Up to nine photos may be sent in a picture message.

Figure 13: Photo Attachment Menu

Figure 14: List of Photo Albums

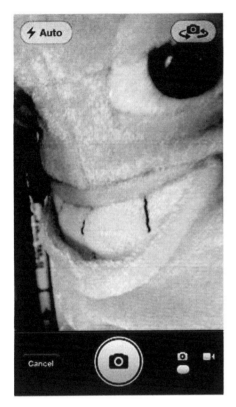

Figure 15: Camera Turned On

11. Sending a Video Message

A video can be attached to any text message. To send a video message:

1. Touch the ⬤ icon at the Home screen. The Messages screen appears.
2. Touch the ✑ icon. The New Message screen appears.
3. Touch the ⬤ button to the left of the text field. The Attachment menu appears.
4. Follow the steps in one of the sections below to either attach an existing video or capture a video to send:

To attach an existing video to the text message:

1. Touch the **Choose Existing** button. The Photo Album appears.
2. Touch a video. The first frame of the video appears. Touch the ▶ button to play a preview of the video.
3. Touch the ▮▮ at the top left of the screen and drag it to the right to trim the beginning of the movie. The beginning of the movie is selected.
4. Touch the ▮▮ at the top right of the screen and drag it to the left to trim the end of the movie. The end of the movie is selected.
5. Touch **Choose**. The video is attached to the text message.

To capture a video and attach it:

1. Touch the **Take Photo or Video** button. The camera turns on.
2. Touch the ⬤■◀ button. The camcorder turns on.
3. Touch the ⬤ button at the bottom of the screen. The camcorder begins to record.
4. Touch the ⬤ button again. The video is captured and stored. The first frame of the new video appears.
5. Touch the ▶ button to preview the video. Trim the video, if needed, as described in steps 3 and 4 of the previous section. Touch **Use**. The video is attached to the text message.

Using the Safari Web Browser

Table of Contents

1. Navigating to a Website

You can surf the Web using your iPhone. To navigate to a website using the Web address:

1. Touch the icon on the Home screen. The Safari Web browser opens.
2. Touch the Address bar at the top of the screen, as outlined in **Figure 1**. The keyboard appears. If you do not see the Address bar, touch the screen and move your finger down to scroll up.
3. Touch the button. The Address field is erased.
4. Type a Web address and touch **Go**. Safari navigates to the website.
5. Touch the button. Safari navigates to the previous Web page.
6. Touch the button. Safari navigates to the next Web page.

Figure 1: Address Bar in Safari

2. Adding and Viewing Bookmarks

The iPhone can store favorite websites as Bookmarks to allow you to access them faster in the future. To add a Bookmark in Safari:

1. Touch the [icon] icon on the Home screen. The Safari browser opens.
2. Navigate to a website. Refer to *"Navigating to a Website"* on page 91 to learn how.

3. Touch the [icon] button at the bottom of the screen. The Sharing menu appears, as shown in **Figure 2**.

4. Touch the [icon] icon. The Add Bookmark window appears, as shown in **Figure 3**.

5. Type a name for the Bookmark, and then touch the [Save] button at the top right of the screen. The website is added to the Bookmarks.

Note: To view saved Bookmarks, touch the [icon] icon at the bottom of the screen in the Safari browser. The Bookmarks screen appears, as shown in **Figure 4**. *Touch a bookmark. Safari navigates to the indicated website.*

Figure 2: Bookmark Menu

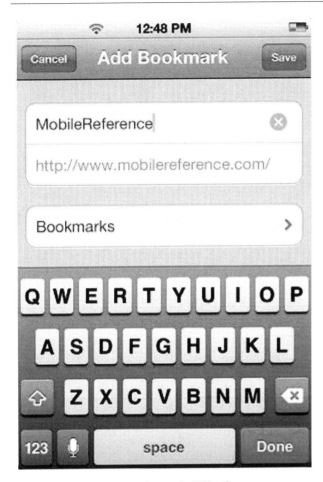

Figure 3: Add Bookmark Window

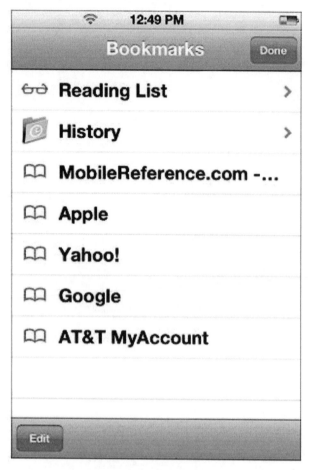

Figure 4: Bookmarks Screen

3. Adding a Bookmark to the Home Screen

On the iPhone, Bookmarks can be added to the Home screen; they will then appear like application icons. To add a Bookmark to the Home screen as an icon:

1. Touch the ![icon] icon on the Home screen. The Safari browser opens.
2. Navigate to a website. Refer to *"Navigating to a Website"* on page 91 to learn how.
3. Touch the ![button] button at the bottom of the screen. The Bookmark menu appears.
4. Touch **Add to Home Screen**. The Add to Home screen appears, as shown in **Figure 5**.
5. Enter a name for the Bookmark and touch the ![Add] button at the top right of the screen. The Bookmark is added to the Home screen.

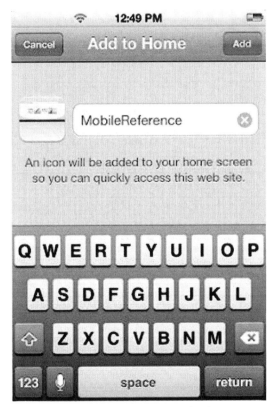

Figure 5: Add to Home Window

4. Managing Open Browser Windows

The Safari Web browser supports up to eight open Browser windows. This feature is analogous to tabbed browsing in a Web browser like Mozilla Firefox or Google Chrome. Use the following tips when working with open Browser windows:

- To view the open Safari windows, touch the button at the bottom right-hand corner of the screen in Safari. The open Safari windows appear, as shown in **Figure 6**.
- Touch the screen and flick your finger to the left or right to view other open windows.

  While viewing the open Safari windows, touch the **New Page** button at the bottom left of the screen. A new Browser window is opened.

- While viewing the open Safari windows, touch the ✖ button at the top left of a page to close it. If there is no ✖ button, then there is only one open window.

Figure 6: Open Safari Windows

5. Blocking Pop-Up Windows

Some websites may have pop-up windows that interfere with browsing the internet. To block pop-ups:

1. Touch the ![icon] icon on the Home screen. The Settings screen appears, as shown in **Figure 7**.
2. Scroll down and touch Safari. The Safari Settings screen appears, as shown in **Figure 8**.
3. Scroll down and touch the ![OFF] switch next to 'Block Pop-Ups'. Pop-ups will now be blocked.
4. Touch the ![ON] switch next to 'Block Pop-Ups'. Pop-ups will now be allowed.

Figure 7: Settings Screen

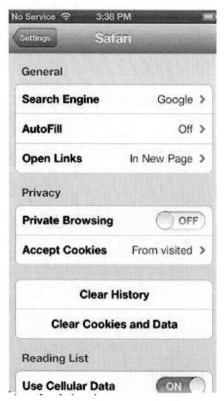

Figure 8: Safari Settings Screen

6. Changing the Search Engine

Google, Yahoo, or Bing can be set as the default search engine in Safari. When you get your new iPhone, the default search engine is set to Google. Touch the text field at the top right of the screen to use the default search engine in Safari, as outlined in **Figure 9**. To change the default search engine:

1. Touch the ![icon] icon on the Home screen. The Settings screen appears.
2. Scroll down and touch **Safari**. The Safari Settings screen appears.
3. Touch **Search Engine**. A list of search engines appears.
4. Touch the preferred search engine. The default search engine is set, and the name of the new search engine will appear in the empty search field in Safari.

Figure 9: Search Field in Safari

7. Clearing the History or Cookies and Data

The iPhone can clear the list of recently visited websites, known as the History, as well as other data, such as saved passwords, known as Cookies. The iPhone can also delete data from previously visited websites. To delete one or both of these items:

1. Touch the ![icon] icon on the Home screen. The Settings screen appears.
2. Scroll down and touch **Safari**. The Safari Settings screen appears.
3. Touch **Clear History** or **Clear Cookies and Data**. A confirmation dialog appears.
4. Touch **Clear History** or **Clear Cookies and Data** again, depending on your selection in step 3. The selected data is deleted and the option is grayed out on the Safari Settings screen.

8. Viewing an Article in Reader Mode

The Safari browser can display certain news articles in Reader Mode, which allows you to read them like a book with no images or links. To view an article in Reader Mode, touch the [Reader] button in the Address bar at any time (when available), as outlined in **Figure 10**. Reader mode turns on, as shown in **Figure 11**. Touch the $_A A$ icon to change the font size.

Figure 10: Reader Button in the Address Bar

Figure 11: Article in Reader Mode

9. Turning Private Browsing On or Off

In order to preserve privacy, the Safari Web browser allows you to surf the Internet without saving the History or any other data showing that you have visited a particular website. To activate Private Browsing:

1. Touch the ![icon] icon on the Home screen. The Settings screen appears.
2. Scroll down and touch **Safari**. The Safari Settings screen appears.
3. Touch the OFF switch next to 'Private Browsing'. Private Browsing is turned on and the Safari colors change to black, as shown in **Figure 12**.
4. Touch the ON switch next to 'Private Browsing'. Private Browsing is turned off.

Figure 12: Private Browsing in Safari

Managing Photos and Videos

Table of Contents

1. Taking a Picture

The iPhone has a built-in eight-megapixel rear-facing camera and a 1.2 megapixel front-facing camera. To take a picture, touch the icon. The camera turns on, as shown in **Figure 1**. Make sure the switch at the bottom right is in the position. Touch the button in the upper right-hand corner of the screen at any time to use the front-facing camera. Aim and touch the

button to take the picture. The shutter closes and opens, and the picture is automatically stored in the 'Camera Roll' album. If the surroundings are too dark, refer to *"Using the Flash"* on page 109 for help.

Note: Refer to "Tips and Tricks" *on page 285 to learn how to take a picture directly from the Lock screen.*

Figure 1: Camera Turned On

2. Capturing a Video

The iPhone has a built-in camcorder that can shoot HD video. To capture a video on the iPhone:

1. Touch the ⬚ icon. The camera turns on, as indicated by the opening shutter animation.
2. Touch the ⬚ switch in the bottom right corner, as outlined in **Figure 2**. The iPhone switches to **Video Capture** mode.
3. Touch the ⬚ button. The camera begins to record.
4. Touch the ⬚ button again. The camera stops recording and the video is automatically saved to the 'Camera Roll' album.

Note: Touch the thumbnail at the bottom left to preview the video.

Figure 2: Video Switch

3. Using the Digital Zoom

While taking pictures, use the camera's built-in Digital Zoom feature if the subject of the photo is far away. Unfortunately, the Digital Zoom will not work when recording videos. To zoom in before taking a photo, touch the screen with two fingers together and move them apart. The appears at the bottom of the screen and the camera zooms in. To zoom out before taking a photo, touch the screen with two fingers apart and move them together. The appears at the bottom of the screen and the camera zooms out.

Note: Because of its digital nature, the zoom function will not provide the best resolution, and the image may look fuzzy. It is recommended to be as close as possible to the subject of the photo.

4. Using the Flash

The iPhone has a built-in LED flash that can be used along with the rear-facing camera. When shooting a video with the flash turned on, it will remain on throughout the movie. To use the flash:

1. Make sure the camera is turned on and the rear camera is activated. Refer to *"Taking a Picture"* on page 106 to learn how.

2. Touch the ⚡ icon at the top left of the screen. The ⚡ Auto | On | Off menu appears.

3. Touch **On**. The flash is turned on permanently.
4. Touch **Off**. The flash is turned off permanently.
5. Touch **Auto**. The flash will be used when needed, as determined by the iPhone's light sensor.

5. Focusing on a Part of the Screen

While taking pictures, the camera can focus on a particular object or area on the screen. This will adjust the lighting and other elements to make the object or area stand out in the picture. To focus on a specific part of the screen, just touch that area. A white box appears and the camera focuses.

6. Browsing Photos

After taking pictures on your iPhone or transferring them from your computer, you may view them at any time. To view saved photos:

1. Touch the ![icon] icon at the Home screen. A list of photo albums appears, as shown in **Figure 3**. The photos you have taken with with the iPhone are in an album called 'Camera Roll'.
2. Touch an album. The photos in the album appear.
3. Touch a photo. The photo appears in full screen.
4. Use the following tips when viewing photos:

   - Touch a photo with your thumb and forefinger and move the two fingers apart to zoom in on it. The zoom will center where your fingers were joined.
   - Touch the screen twice quickly to zoom out completely.
   - Touch the photo with your thumb and forefinger spread apart and move the fingers together while touching the photo to zoom out gradually.
   - Move your fingers apart to zoom in.
   - Touch the album name at the top left of the screen while viewing a photo to return to album view. If the album name is not shown, touch the photo once to make the Photo menus appear at the top and bottom of the screen.

   - Touch the ▷ icon at the bottom of the screen while viewing a photo to start a slideshow of photos in that album.

Figure 3: List of Photo Albums

7. Editing a Photo

The iPhone provides basic photo-editing tools. To edit a photo:

1. Touch the [icon] icon at the Home screen. A list of photo albums appears.
2. Touch an album. The photos in the album appear.
3. Touch a photo. The photo appears in full screen.
4. Touch the **Edit** button in the upper right-hand corner of the screen. The Photo Editing menu appears at the bottom of the screen, as shown in **Figure 4**. If the button is not visible, touch the screen once to make the Photo menus appear at the top and bottom of the screen.
5. Touch one of the following icons to edit the photo:

   - [icon] - Rotates the photo 90 degrees counter-clockwise. Touch repeatedly to keep rotating the photo. Touch the **Save** button in the upper right-hand corner of the screen to save the changes.

   - [icon] - Enhances the quality of the photo. Touch the **Save** button in the upper right-hand corner of the screen to save the changes.

   - [icon] - Removes red-eye from the photo. Touch each red eye in the photo and then touch the **Apply** button in the upper right-hand corner of the screen to save the changes.

   - [icon] - Crops the photo. Touch the corners of the photo and drag the selected portion, as shown in **Figure 5**. Touch **Constrain** at the bottom of the screen and touch a size to choose a specific crop dimension. Touch the **Crop** button in the upper right-hand corner of the screen to save the changes.

Figure 4: Photo Editing Menu

Figure 5: Cropping a Photo

8. Deleting a Photo

You may delete unwanted pictures from your iPhone to free up memory. To delete a photo:

Warning: Once a picture is deleted, there is no way to restore it.

1. Touch the icon. A list of photo albums appears.
2. Touch an album. The photos contained in the album appear.
3. Touch a photo. The photo appears in full screen view.
4. Touch the button in the lower right-hand corner of the screen. The Delete menu appears, as shown in **Figure 6**, if the photo only exists in one album. The Delete Everywhere menu appears, as shown in **Figure 7**, if the photo exists in two or more albums. The Remove from Album menu appears, as shown in **Figure 8**, if it is being deleted from an album to which it is copied.
5. Touch **Delete Photo**, **Delete from Album**, or **Delete Everywhere**. The photo is deleted from the iPhone or specifed location.

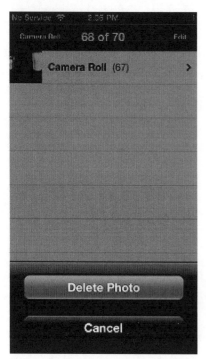

Figure 6: Delete Menu

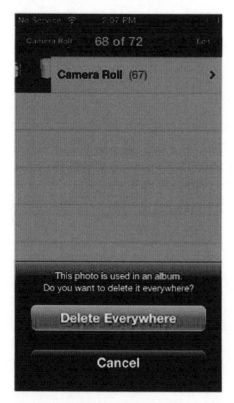

Figure 7: Delete Everywhere Menu

Figure 8: Remove from Album Menu

9. Creating a Photo Album

You can create a photo album right from your iPhone. To create a photo album:

1. Touch the [icon] icon. A list of photo albums appears.
2. Touch the **Edit** button in the upper right-hand corner of the screen. The Album menu appears at the top of the screen, as shown in **Figure 9**.
3. Touch the **+** button in the upper left-hand corner. The New Album window appears, as shown in **Figure 10**.
4. Type a name for the album and touch **Save**. The new photo album is created and you can now choose photos to add to it.
5. Touch a photo album and then touch photos to add them to the new album. Touch a photo a second time to deselect it. Touch the **Albums** button in the upper left-hand corner of the screen at any time to return to the album list.
6. Touch the **Done** button in the upper right-hand corner of the screen. The selected photos are added to the new photo album.

Figure 9: Album Menu

Figure 10: New Album Window

10. Editing a Photo Album

Photo albums stored on the iPhone can be edited right from your device. Refer to *"Creating a Photo Album"* on page 118 to learn how to make a new photo album using your phone.

To edit the name of a photo album:

1. Touch the  icon. A list of photo albums appears.
2. Touch the **Edit** button in the upper right-hand corner of the screen. The Album menu appears.
3. Touch the name of a photo album. The virtual keyboard appears.
4. Type a new name for the album. The new album name is entered.
5. Touch the **Done** button in the upper right-hand corner of the screen. The album is renamed.

To add photos to an album:

1. Touch the icon. A list of photo albums appears.
2. Touch an album. The photos contained in the album appear.
3. Touch the **Edit** button in the upper right-hand corner of the screen. Photos can now be selected.
4. Touch as many photos as desired. The photos are selected and ✓ icons appear on the thumbnails, as shown in **Figure 11**.
5. Touch the **Add To** button at the bottom of the screen. The Add To menu appears, as shown in **Figure 12**.
6. Touch **Add to Existing Album**. A list of photo albums appears.
7. Touch the name of a photo album. The selected photos are added to the album.

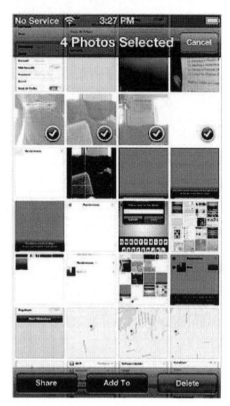

Figure 11: Selected Photos

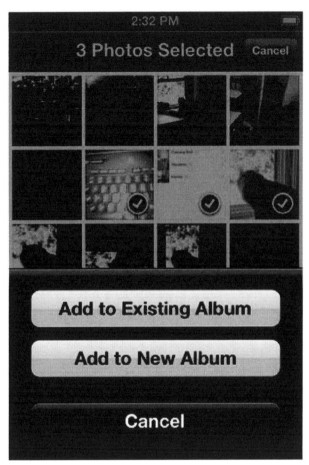

Figure 12: Add To Menu

11. Deleting a Photo Album

Photo albums stored on the iPhone can be deleted right from your phone. To delete a photo album:

Warning: When an album is deleted from the iPhone, any photos that are stored in other albums will remain on the iPhone. Make sure any photos you wish to keep are stored in another album. Refer to* "Editing a Photo Album" *on page 121 to learn how to add photos to an album.

1. Touch the ![icon] icon. A list of photo albums appears.

2. Touch the **Edit** button in the upper right-hand corner of the screen. The Album menu appears.

3. Touch the ![button] button to the left of an album. The **Delete** button appears next to the album.

4. Touch the **Delete** button. A confirmation appears at the bottom of the screen.

5. Touch **Delete Album**. The photo album is deleted. Touch the **Done** button to return to the Album menu.

12. Starting a Slideshow

The iPhone can play a slideshow using the photos in your albums. To begin a slideshow:

1. Touch the ![icon] icon. A list of photo albums appears.
2. Touch an album. The photos in the album appear.
3. Touch a photo. The photo appears in Full Screen.
4. Touch the ▶ button at the bottom of the screen. The Slideshow Settings screen appears, as shown in **Figure 13**. If the ▶ button is not visible, touch the screen once to make the Photo menus appear.
5. Touch **Transitions** and select the transition for the slideshow. Touch the **Slideshow Options** button to return to the Slideshow Settings screen.
6. Touch the **OFF** switch next to 'Play Music' and then touch **Music** to select a song to play during the slideshow. Touch the **Start Slideshow** button when ready. The slideshow begins, showing all photos in the selected album.

Figure 13: Slideshow Settings Screen

13. Saving a Picture from a Picture Message

After receiving a picture as an attachment in a text message, you may save it to a photo album. To save a picture from a picture message:

1. Touch the ⬜ icon. The Messages screen appears, as shown in **Figure 14**.
2. Touch the conversation that contains the picture. The Conversation screen appears.
3. Touch the photo in the conversation. The photo appears in full-screen view.
4. Touch the ⬜ icon. The Save Photo menu appears, as shown in **Figure 15**.
5. Touch **Save Image**. The photo is saved to the iPhone. By default, the photo is stored in the 'Camera Roll' album.

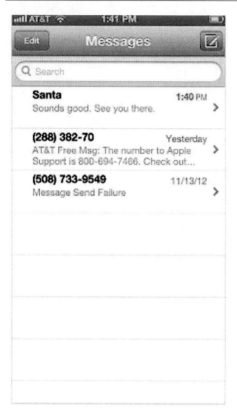

Figure 14: Messages Screen

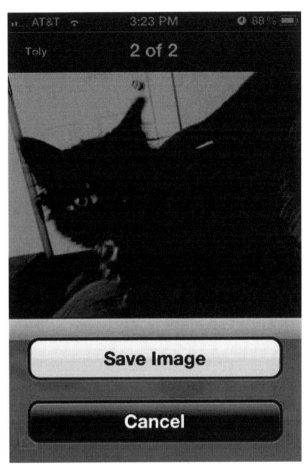

Figure 15: Save Photo Menu

14. Using the Places Feature

The iPhone can display a map within the photos application, which shows an overview of the physical locations of the photos captured on the phone. The first time you use your camera, touch **OK** when the iPhone asks whether to turn on Location Services. To use Places:

1. Touch the icon. A list of photo albums appears.
2. Touch **Places** in the lower right-hand corner of the screen. A map appears, as shown in **Figure 16**.
3. Touch the screen with your thumb and forefinger and move them apart. The map zooms in, as shown in **Figure 17**. The markers indicate the exact locations where photos were taken.
4. Touch a marker. The number of photos in that location is displayed, as shown in **Figure 18**.
5. Touch the button. The selected photos are displayed.

Note: Touch the ALBUMS icon at the bottom left of the screen to return to your albums.

Figure 16: Map in Places (zoomed out)

Figure 17: Map in Places (zoomed in)

Figure 18: Number of Photos in a Places Location

Using iTunes on the iPhone

Table of Contents

1. Setting Up an iTunes Account

In order to buy content, you will need to have an iTunes account. Refer to *"Setting Up an iTunes Account"* on page 131 to learn more.

2. Buying Music in iTunes

Music can be purchased directly from the iPhone via iTunes. To buy music using the iTunes application:

1. Touch the ![icon] icon. The iTunes application opens.
2. Touch the ![icon] icon in the bottom left-hand corner. The iTunes Music Store opens and the new releases are shown.
3. Touch **Featured**, **Charts**, or **Genres** at the top of the screen to browse music. The corresponding section appears.
4. Touch an album. The Album description appears, as shown in **Figure 1**.
5. Touch the price of the album. 'Buy Album' appears.
6. Touch **Buy Album**. The album is purchased. Alternatively, touch the price of a song and then touch **Buy Song** to buy a single song.
7. Touch the ![icon] icon at the bottom right of the screen to view the download progress. Touch **Downloads**. The Downloads screen appears, as shown in **Figure 2**. If the list is empty, all downloads are complete.

Note: Depending on your settings, you may need to enter your iTunes password when purchasing music on the iPhone.

Figure 1: Album Description

Figure 2: Downloads Screen

3. Buying or Renting Videos in iTunes

Videos can be purchased or rented directly from the iPhone and viewed using the iPod application. To buy videos using the iTunes application:

1. Touch the ⊙ icon. The iTunes application opens.

2. Touch the ▢ icon or the ▦ icon at the bottom of the screen. The iTunes TV Show or Movie store opens, depending on your selection, and the new releases appear (movies), as shown in **Figure 3**.
3. Touch a video. The Video description appears, as shown in **Figure 4**.
4. Touch the price of the movie.'Buy Movie' or 'Rent Movie' appears, depending on your selection.
5. Touch BUY MOVIE or $4.99 RENT (where the price varies based on the video). The iPhone may ask for your iTunes password. The video is purchased or rented and the download begins.
6. Touch the ● ● ● icon in the lower right-hand corner of the screen to view the download progress. Touch **Downloads**. The Downloads screen appears. If the list is empty, the downloads are already complete.

Note: When renting a video, the video is available for 24 hours once you start watching it. Once 24 hours has passed since you began to play the video, you will not be able to resume the video if you pause it.

Figure 3: iTunes Video Store

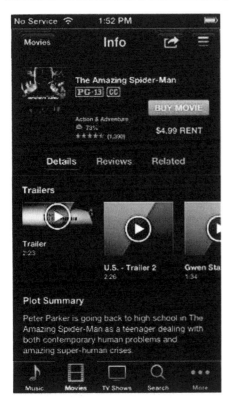

Figure 4: Video Description

4. Buying Tones in iTunes

Ringtones can be purchased directly from your iPhone to use for incoming calls. To buy ringtones using the iTunes application:

1. Touch the [icon] icon. The iTunes application opens.
2. Touch the [icon] icon at the bottom right-hand corner of the screen. The More screen appears, as shown in **Figure 5**.
3. Touch **Tones**. The iTunes Tone Store opens, as shown in **Figure 6**.
4. Touch **FEATURED**, **CHARTS**, or **GENRES** at the top of the screen to browse ringtones. Touch a ringtone. The Ringtone Information screen appears, as shown in **Figure 7**.
5. Touch the name of the ringtone under 'Songs'. A preview of the ringtone plays.
6. Touch the price of the ringtone. 'Buy Now' appears.
7. Touch **BUY NOW**. The Assign Ringtone window appears, as shown in **Figure 8**.
8. Touch **Set as Default** or **Assign To Contact**. The ringtone is purchased, downloaded to the iPhone, and set as the corresponding ringtone. Alternatively, touch **Done** to just purchase the ringtone without setting it.
9. Touch the [icon] icon to view the download progress. Touch **Downloads**. The Downloads screen appears. If the list is empty, the downloads are already complete.

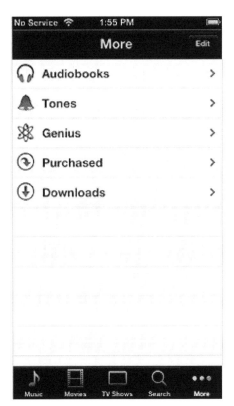

Figure 5: More Screen

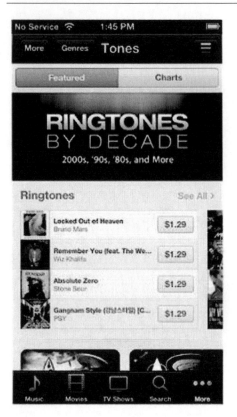

Figure 6: iTunes Tone Store

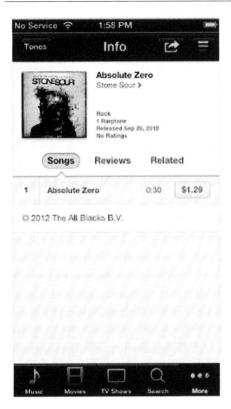

Figure 7: Ringtone Information Screen

\

Figure 8: Assign Ringtone Window

5. Searching for Media in iTunes

The iPhone can search for any media in the iTunes Store. To search for media:

1. Touch the ⊙ icon. The iTunes application opens.
2. Touch the 🔍 icon at the bottom of the screen. The search field appears in the upper right-hand corner of the screen. Touch the field and then touch the ⊗ button at the top right of the screen to clear it.
3. Type the name of a song, video, or other media that you wish to find. Touch **Search**. The available results appear, organized by the type of media, as shown in **Figure 9**.
4. Touch a song, video, or other media. The Media description appears. If you touch the name of an eBook, the View in iBooks window appears, as shown in **Figure 10**.

Note: Refer to "Buying Music in iTunes" on page 132, "Buying or Renting Videos in iTunes" on page 135, or "Buying Tones in iTunes" on page 138 to learn how to purchase media.

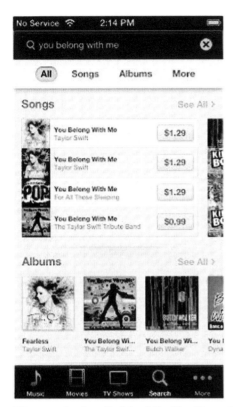

Figure 9: Available Media Results

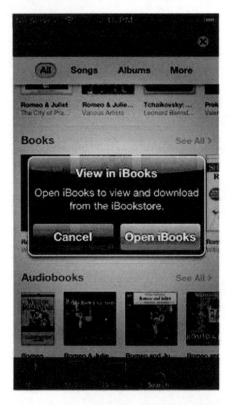

Figure 10: View in iBooks Window

6. Playing Media

To play media that was purchased in iTunes on the iPhone, use the Music Application. To learn how, refer to *"Using the Music Application"* on page 145.

Using the Music Application

Table of Contents

1. Downloading Media

Use the iTunes Application to download media to the iPhone. Refer to *"Using iTunes on the iPhone"* on page 131 to learn how.

2. Playing Music

The Music application on the iPhone can be used to play music. To listen to your music:

1. Touch the ![icon] icon. The Music application opens.
2. Touch one of the following icons at the bottom of the screen to browse music:

   - ![icon] - Browse existing playlists or add a playlist.
   - ![icon] - Browse existing artists.
   - ![icon] - Browse existing songs.
   - ![icon] - Browse existing albums.

3. Use the following tips to navigate the Music Application:
   - Touch a playlist, artist, or song to play the item. The item plays, as shown in **Figure 1**.
   - Tilt the iPhone horizontally. The available albums appear in Album view, as shown in **Figure 2**.
   - Touch the screen and drag your finger to the left or right while the iPhone is horizontal. Other albums appear.

*Note: The music keeps playing after returning to the Home screen or switching to another application. The music can be controlled without returning to the Music application; just press the **Home** button twice and then swipe the application icons at the bottom of the screen to the right until the Music controls appear, as shown in **Figure 3**. Also, press the Home button twice while the iPhone is locked to bring up the Music controls, as shown in **Figure 4**. Press the **Home** button twice again to hide the music controls.*

Figure 1: Music Playing

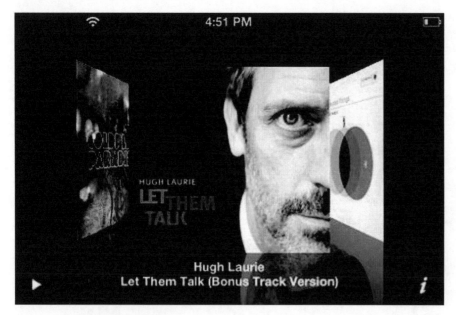

Figure 2: Album View

Figure 3: Music Controls

Figure 4: Music Controls on the Lock Screen

3. Using Additional Audio Controls

To view the controls while listening to music, touch the album art once. The Song Controls appear, as shown in **Figure 5**. Touch one of the following to perform the corresponding function:

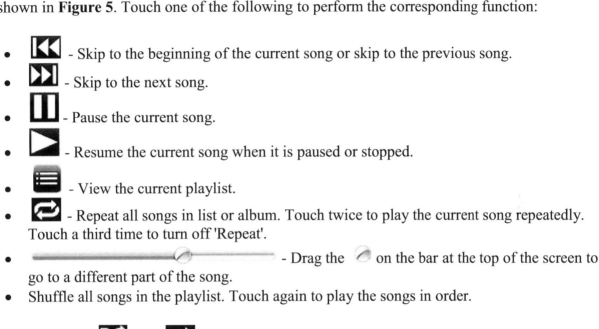

- - Skip to the beginning of the current song or skip to the previous song.
- - Skip to the next song.
- - Pause the current song.
- - Resume the current song when it is paused or stopped.
- - View the current playlist.
- - Repeat all songs in list or album. Touch twice to play the current song repeatedly. Touch a third time to turn off 'Repeat'.
- - Drag the on the bar at the top of the screen to go to a different part of the song.
- Shuffle all songs in the playlist. Touch again to play the songs in order.

Note: Touch both and to play songs continuously in random order. To shuffle and play all songs, go to the song list and touch the icon.

Figure 5: Song Controls

4. Creating and Editing a Playlist

Playlists can be created in iTunes on your computer. However, the Music application can perform the same function. To create a playlist in the Music application:

1. Touch the ![icon] icon in the Music application. The existing playlists appear.
2. Touch **Add Playlist**. The New Playlist window appears, as shown in **Figure 6**.
3. Type the name of the playlist and touch **Save**. A list of the songs on your iPhone appears, as shown in **Figure 7**.
4. Touch one of the icons at the bottom of the screen to browse music to add to the new playlist. Refer to *"Playing Music"* on page 146 to learn more about finding music in the Music application.

5. Touch a song. The song is grayed out and added to the playlist. Touch **Add All Albums** when browsing artists to add all music by an artist, or touch **Add All Songs** when browsing songs to add all of your music to the playlist, or touch **Add All Songs** when viewing an album to add all music form that album.

6. Touch the [Done] button in the upper right-hand corner of the screen. The playlist is populated with the selected music. After creating a playlist, you can add or remove music from it.

To edit a playlist:

1. Touch the [icon] icon in the Music application. The available playlists appear.
2. Touch a playlist. The Playlist screen appears, as shown in **Figure 8**.

3. Touch **Edit**. The [−] button appears next to every song in the playlist.

4. Touch the [−] button. The [Delete] button appears next to the selected song.

5. Touch the [Delete] button. The song is removed from the playlist.

6. Touch the [+] button at the top left of the screen to add songs. To add songs, repeat steps 4 and 5 from the previous instructions. The selected songs are added to the playlist.

7. Touch the [Done] button. The changes to the playlist are saved.

Note: Removing a song from a playlist will not delete it from the Music library.

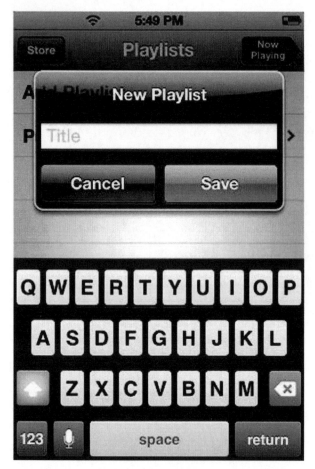

Figure 6: New Playlist Window

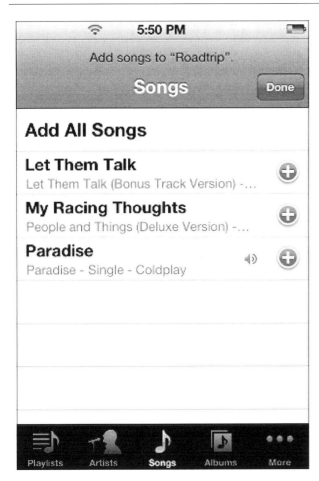

Figure 7: List of Songs on Your iPhone

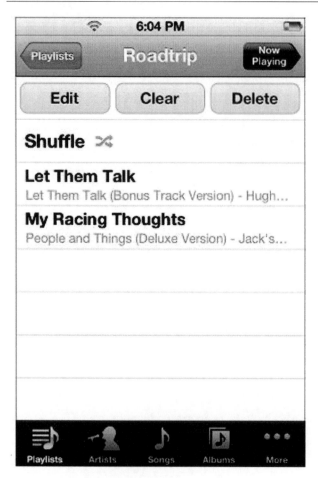

Figure 8: Playlist Screen

Using the Email Application

Table of Contents

1. Setting Up the Email Application

Before the Email application can be used, at least one account must be set up on your iPhone. To set up the Email application:

1. Touch the ![icon] icon. The Settings screen appears, as shown in **Figure 1**.
2. Scroll down and touch Mail, Contacts, Calendars. The Mail, Contacts, Calendars screen appears, as shown in **Figure 2**.
3. Touch **Add Account**. The Account Type screen appears, as shown in **Figure 3**.
4. Touch one of the following to select a mail service and set up an email account:

   - **Microsoft Exchange** – Refer to *"Setting Up Microsoft Exchange"* on page 160 to learn how to set up an Exchange email account.
   - **Gmail, mobileme, Yahoo Mail, AOL** – Refer to *"Setting Up mobileme, Gmail, Yahoo, Hotmail, or AOL"* on page 161 to learn how to set up one of these email accounts.
   - **Other** – Refer to *"Setting Up a Different Service"* on page 162 to learn how set up another service.

Figure 1: Settings Screen

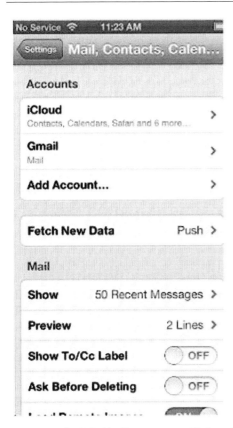

Figure 2: Mail, Contacts, Calendars Screen

Figure 3: Account Type Screen

Setting Up Microsoft Exchange

To set up a Microsoft Exchange account:

1. Touch **Microsoft Exchange**. The Exchange screen appears, as shown in **Figure 4**.
2. Touch each field and type the required information. The information is entered.
3. Touch the [Next] button at the top right-hand corner of the screen. The iPhone verifies your information and, provided that everything is correct, the Mail, Contacts, Calendars screen appears. Your Microsoft Exchange account is now setup.

Figure 4: Exchange Screen

Setting Up mobileMe, Gmail, Yahoo mail, Hotmail, or AOL

To set up a mobileme, Gmail, Yahoo, or AOL account:

1. Touch **mobileme**, **Gmail**, **Yahoo Mail**, or **AOL**. The Account Information screen appears, as shown in **Figure 5** (Gmail).
2. Touch each field and type the required information. The information is entered.
3. Touch the ___Save___ button. The iPhone verifies your information and, provided that everything is correct, the Mail, Contacts, Calendars screen appears. Your email account is setup.

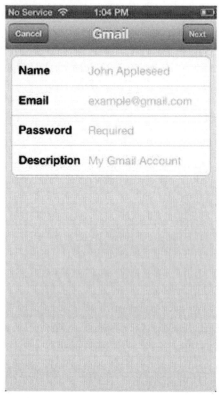

Figure 5: Account Information Screen

Setting Up a Different Service

To set up an account other than the ones listed above:

1. Touch **Other**. The Other Account screen appears, as shown in **Figure 6**.
2. Touch a type of account. The Account Information screen appears.
3. Touch each field and type the required information. Touch the ![Save] or ![Next] button at the top right-hand corner of the screen when all required fields are filled in.
4. The iPhone verifies your information and, provided that everything is correct, the Mail, Contacts, Calendars screen appears. Your email account is setup.

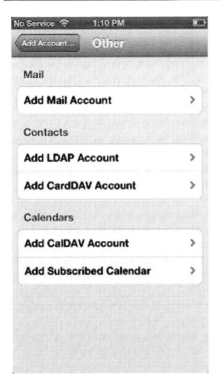

Figure 6: Other Account Screen

2. Reading Email

You can read your email on the iPhone via the Email application. Before opening the Email application, make sure that you have set up your email account. Refer to *"Setting Up the Email Application"* on page 157 to learn how. To read your email:

1. Touch the ▢ icon. The Email application opens and the Inbox appears, as shown in **Figure 7**. If the email messages are not shown, touch Inbox on the mailboxes screen or at the top left-hand corner of the screen if the name of your email is shown. This is the same name that you gave the account when setting it up.
2. Touch a message. The message appears.
3. Touch **Inbox** in the upper left-hand corner of the screen in an email to return to the list of received messages. Touch **Mailboxes** in the upper left-hand corner of the screen in the list of messages to return to the list of mailboxes. The mailbox list varies depending on the mail service.

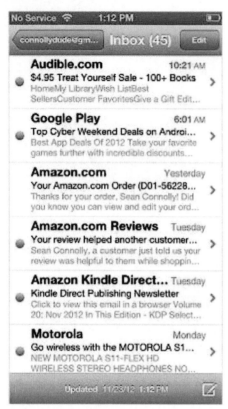

Figure 7: Other Account Screen

3. Switching Accounts in the Email Application

If you have more than one active email account, you can switch between them or view all of your email in one Inbox. To switch to another account:

1. Touch the ![icon] icon. The Email application opens and your emails appear.
2. Touch the name of the email account at the top left-hand corner of the screen, which is the same name that you gave the account when setting it up. A list of folders appears, as shown in **Figure 8**. Refer to *"Setting Up the Email Application"* on page 157 to learn more.
3. Touch the **Mailboxes** button at the top left-hand corner of the screen. A list of all active inboxes and accounts appears, as shown in **Figure 9**.
4. Touch an account. The folders for that account appear.
5. Touch **Inbox**. The emails in the Inbox appear.

*Note: You can also touch **All Inboxes** to view emails from all of the accounts attached to your iPhone in a single, joint folder.*

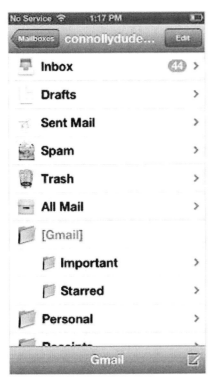

Figure 8: List of Folders

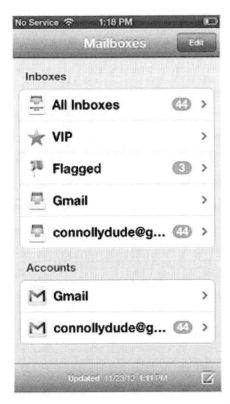

Figure 9: List of Active Inboxes and Accounts

4. Writing an Email

You can write and send emails directly from your iPhone. To write and send an email:

1. Touch the ⬚ icon. The Email application opens.

2. Touch the ⬚ button at the bottom right of the screen. The New Message screen appears, as shown in **Figure 10**.

3. Start typing the name of a contact. A list of matching contacts appears below as you type.

4. Touch the name of the contact that you wish to email. The contact's email is added to the addressee list. Alternatively, type an email address from scratch. Enter as many additional addressees as desired.

5. Touch the text field to the right of 'Subject:' and enter a topic for the message. The subject is entered.

6. Touch the **return** button at the bottom right of the keyboard. The cursor jumps to the body of the email.

7. Type the email. The text is entered in the email. To use numbers or symbols, touch the **123** button at the bottom left-hand corner of the keyboard. To use other symbols, touch the **#+=** button at the bottom left-hand corner of the keyboard after touching the **123** button.

8. Touch the **Send** button at the top right-hand corner of the screen. The email is sent.

Note: If you exit the eMail application before touching the **Send** *button, the iPhone will ask if you would like to save the draft. Saved drafts can be viewed in the 'Drafts' folder.*

Figure 10: New Message Screen

5. Formatting Text

When writing an email on your iPhone, you can format the text to add bold, italics, or underline, or you can increase the quote level.

To add bold, italics, or underline to text while writing an email:

1. Touch and hold the text that you wish to format. The Select menu appears above the text, as shown in **Figure 11**.
2. Touch **Select All**. All of the text is selected. To select a single word, touch **Select**. Blue dots appear on either side of the selected word or phrase.
3. Touch and hold one of the blue dots and drag it in any direction. The text between the dots is highlighted and a Text menu appears, as shown in **Figure 12**.
4. Touch the [B I U] button. The 'Bold', 'Italics', and 'Underline' buttons appear. If you cannot see the [B I U] button, touch the [▶] button to view more options. The Text Format menu appears, as shown in **Figure 13**.
5. Touch one of the buttons. The associated formatting is applied to the selected text. You can also increase the left margin, or quote level, in an email.

To increase the quote level:

1. Touch and hold text in your email. The Select menu appears above the text.
2. Touch the [▶] button in the Text menu. The Quote Level button appears.
3. Touch the **Quote Level** button. The Quote Level options appear.
4. Touch the **Decrease** or **Increase** button to adjust the Quote Level. The new Quote Level is set and applied to the entire email.

Figure 11: Select Menu

Figure 12: Text Menu

Figure 13: Text Format Menu

6. Replying to and Forwarding Email Messages

After receiving an email, you can reply to the sender or forward the email to a new recipient. To reply to, or forward, an email message:

1. Touch the ⊠ icon. The Email application opens.
2. Touch an email. The body of the email appears.

3. Touch the ↰ icon at the bottom of the screen. The Reply menu appears, as shown in **Figure 14**.
4. Touch **Reply** to reply to the message or touch **Forward** to forward the message. The New Message screen appears. The subject at the top is preceded by 'Re:' if replying or 'Fwd:' if forwarding. The original email is copied in the body. If replying, the addressee field is filled in.
5. Touch the text field next to 'To:' and enter an addressee, if necessary. The addressee is entered.
6. Touch the text field to the right of 'Subject' to enter a different subject for your message, if desired. The subject is entered.
7. Touch the text field below 'Subject' and type a message, if desired. The message is entered.

8. Touch the **Send** button at the top right-hand corner of the screen. The email is sent.

Figure 14: Reply Menu

7. Deleting Emails

You may archive emails from your Inbox to free up space and improve organization. Archiving emails moves them to a folder that does not take up space on your phone, which is equivalent to deleting them. To archive an email:

1. Touch the icon. The Email application opens. It may take a few moments to connect and receive the email messages.

2. Touch an email in the list and drag your finger to the left. The **Archive** button appears to the right of the email.

3. Touch the **Archive** button. The email is sent to the Archive folder and disappears from the Inbox.

*Note: Touch the name of your email account in the upper left-hand corner of the screen and then touch **All Mail** to view all emails, including those that have been archived.*

8. Changing the Default Signature

The iPhone can set a default signature, which will be attached to the end of each email that is sent from the phone. To set or change this signature:

1. Touch the ![icon] icon. The Settings screen appears.
2. Scroll down and touch **Mail, Contacts, Calendars**. The Mail, Contacts, Calendars screen appears.
3. Scroll down and touch **Signature**. The Signature screen appears, as shown in **Figure 15**. Touch **All Accounts** or **Per Account** depending on your preference.
4. Enter a signature in the 'Signature' field at the bottom of the screen, or in each field under each specific account. To use numbers or symbols, touch the ![123] button at the bottom left-hand corner of the keyboard. To use other symbols, touch the ![#+=] button at the bottom left of the screen after touching the ![123] button.
5. Touch the **Mail** button in the upper left-hand corner of the screen when finished. The new signature is saved.

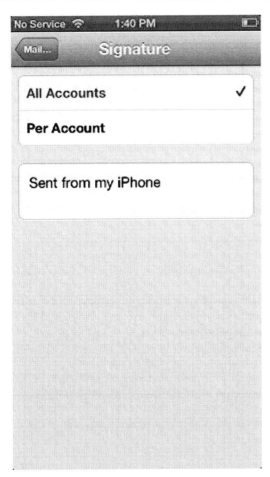

Figure 15: Signature Screen

9. Changing How You Receive Email

There are two options for receiving email on the iPhone. The iPhone can check for new email only when you launch the Email application, or it can constantly check for email and display an alert when a new email arrives. To set the iPhone to check for email either at regular intervals or only when the Email application is launched:

1. Touch the icon. The Settings screen appears.
2. Scroll down and touch **Mail, Contacts, Calendars**. The Mail, Contacts, Calendars screen appears.
3. Touch **Fetch New Data**. The Fetch screen appears, as shown in **Figure 16**.
4. Touch **Advanced**. The Advanced screen appears, as shown in **Figure 17**.
5. Touch an email account. The Account screen appears.
6. Touch **Manual**. A check mark appears next to 'Manual' and the iPhone will now check for new email only when the Email application is opened.
7. Touch **Fetch**. A check mark appears next to 'Fetch' and the iPhone will now check for new email at regular intervals, which can be set at the Fetch screen.

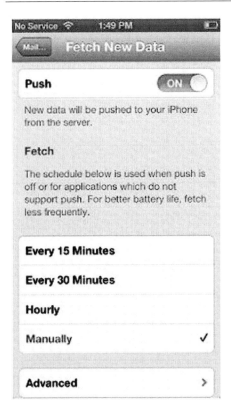

Figure 16: Fetch Screen

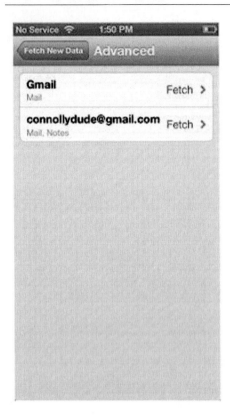

Figure 17: Advanced Screen

10. Changing Email Options

There are various options that change the way that your Email application works. Touch the icon and then touch **Mail, Contacts, Calendars** to change one of the following options:

- **Show** - Choose how many email messages the Email application displays at one time.
- **Preview** - Choose the number of lines of an email message to preview in the Inbox.
- **Show To/Cc Label** – Choose whether to hide the 'To' and 'Cc' labels and show only addresses.
- **Ask Before Deleting** – Choose whether to display a confirmation before deleting an email.
  Load Remote Images - Choose whether to load image attachments in an email automatically.
- **Organize by Thread** – Choose whether to group all emails with the same contact as a conversation.
- **Increase Quote Level** - Choose whether to increase the left margin when replying to or forwarding an email.
- **Default Account** - Choose the account to use as the 'From' address when sending an email from outside of the Email application.

Managing Applications

Table of Contents

1. Setting Up an iTunes Account

In order to buy applications, you will need to have an iTunes account. To set up a new iTunes account:

1. Touch the ![icon] icon. The Settings screen appears, as shown in **Figure 1**.
2. Scroll down and touch **iTunes & App Stores**. The iTunes & Store Settings screen appears, as shown in **Figure 2**.
3. Enter your Apple ID and password, and touch Sign In. Your Apple ID is added to the iPhone.
4. Touch **Create New Apple ID**. The New Account screen appears, as shown in **Figure 3**.
5. Touch **United States**. A list of countries appears.
6. Touch the country where you live and touch the **Done** button. The country is selected.
7. Touch the **Next** button in the lower right-hand corner of the screen. The iTunes agreement screen appears.
8. Read the agreement and touch **Agree**. An acknowledgement dialog appears.
9. Touch **Agree**. The Account screen appears.
10. Touch each field and type the required information. Touch the **Next** button at the bottom right-hand corner of the screen. The next Account Creation screen appears.
11. Touch each field and type your credit card information. Touch the **Next** button. Your account is created, and the account is assigned to the iPhone.

Note: You do not require an Apple ID in order to install free applications.

Figure 1: Settings Screen

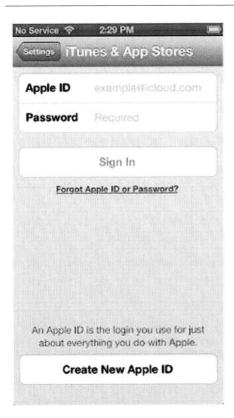

Figure 2: iTunes & Store Settings Screen

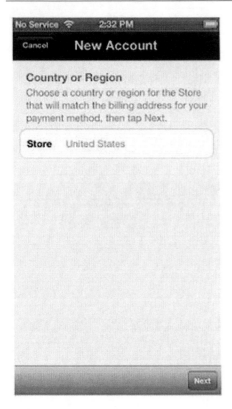

Figure 3: New Account Screen

2. Signing In to a Different iTunes Account

If more than one person uses your iPhone, you may wish to sign in with an alternate Apple ID. Only one Apple ID may be signed in at a time. To sign out and sign in to a different iTunes account:

1. Touch the [icon] icon. The Settings screen appears.
2. Scroll down and touch **iTunes & App Stores**. The Store screen appears. If someone is signed in to their iTunes account on the iPhone, their email account appears as a button at the top of the screen.
3. Touch the email at the top of the screen. The Apple ID window appears, as shown in **Figure 4**.
4. Touch **Sign Out**. The account is signed out.
5. Enter your account information, and then touch **Sign In**. Your account is registered to your iPhone. Alternatively, touch **Create New Apple ID**. Refer to *"Setting Up an iTunes Account"* on page 131 to learn how to create a new iTunes account.

Figure 4: Sign In Window

3. Editing iTunes Account Information

You must keep your account information up to date in order to purchase applications from the iTunes Application Store. For instance, when your billing address changes or your credit card expires, you must change your information. To edit iTunes account information:

1. Touch the ![icon] icon. The Settings screen appears.
2. Scroll down and touch **iTunes & App Stores**. The Store screen appears.
3. Touch **Sign In** and **Use Existing Apple ID** if you are not signed in. Enter your registered email and password and touch **OK**. You are signed in.
4. Touch your email at the top of the screen. The Apple ID window appears.
5. Touch **View Apple ID**. The iPhone requires you to re-enter your password. Type your registered password and touch **OK**. The Account Screen appears with your personal account information.
6. Touch a field to edit it, and then touch the ![Done] button at the top right of the screen. The new information is saved.

4. Searching for an Application

Use the Application Store to search for applications. There are three ways to search for applications:

Manual Search

To search for an application manually:

1. Touch the icon. The Application Store opens, as shown in **Figure 5**.
2. Touch the button at the bottom of the screen. The Search field appears at the top of the screen, as outlined in **Figure 6**.
3. Touch the Search field at the top of the screen. The virtual keyboard appears at the bottom of the screen.
4. Type the name of an application and touch **Search** in the lower right-hand corner of the screen. All matching results appears.

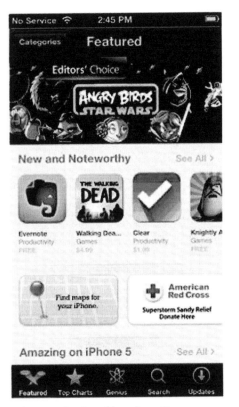

Figure 5: Application Store

Figure 6: Search Field in the Application Store

Browse by Category

To browse applications by category:

1. Touch the icon. The Application Store opens.
2. Touch **Featured** or **Top Charts** at the top of the screen, and then touch Categories at the top left-hand corner of the screen. The Categories screen appears, as shown in **Figure 7**. Touch the screen and move your finger up or down to scroll through the categories.
3. Touch a category to browse it. Some categories have sub-categories. Repeat step 2 to find the sub-category you need.

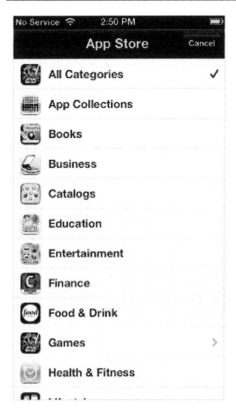

Figure 7: Categories Screen

Browse by Popularity

To browse applications by popularity:

1. Touch the ![icon] icon. The Application Store opens.
2. Touch the ![icon] icon at the bottom of the screen. The Top Charts screen appears, as shown in **Figure 8**.
3. Touch one of the following to browse the applications in the category:

   - **Paid** - View the most popular paid applications.
   - **Free** - View the most popular free applications.
   - **Top Grossing** - View the most popular applications that have earned their creators the most money.

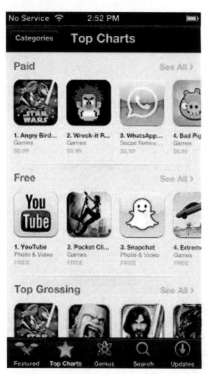

Figure 8: Top Charts Screen

5. Buying an Application

You may purchase applications directly from your iPhone. To buy an application:

1. Touch the ![icon] icon. The Application Store opens.
2. Find an application. Refer to *"Searching for an Application"* on page 186 to learn how.
3. Touch an application in the list. The Application description appears, as shown in **Figure 9**.
4. Touch the price or the word 'Free' in the upper right-hand corner of the screen. **BUY APP** appears if the application is paid or **INSTALL APP** appears if the application is free. If the application is already downloaded to your iPhone, 'INSTALLED' appears at the top right. Touch the **BUY APP** or **INSTALL APP** button. The password prompt appears.
5. Type your iTunes password and touch **OK**. The application is downloaded and installed.

Figure 9: Application Description

6. Using iTunes to Download an Application from a Computer

You may also use iTunes on your computer to purchase and download applications for your iPhone in case your iPhone is not accessible. To use iTunes to purchase and download applications from your computer:

1. Install iTunes. Go to **www.itunes.com/download** to download it. Click **Download Now** and follow the on-screen instructions. iTunes downloads and installs.
2. Open iTunes and connect the iPhone to your computer using the provided USB cable. This is the same cable used to charge your iPhone. Unplug the USB end from the power adapter and plug that end into a USB port on your computer. Make sure the iPhone is on. 'Sync in Progress' appears on the iPhone.
3. The first time the iPhone is connected, iTunes will ask you to register. You can do this later. Just click **Register Later** or **Never Register** to ignore this.
4. Click **iTunes Store** on the left side of the screen. The iTunes store opens, as shown in **Figure 10**.
5. Click **App Store** at the top of the page. The Application Store opens.
6. Click **Search Store** in the upper right-hand corner of the screen and type in an application name or keyword. Available results appear.

7. Click the name of an application. The Application description appears, as shown in **Figure 11**.
8. Click **Buy App**. The iTunes Sign In dialog appears.
9. Type in your registered email address and password and click **Buy**. A confirmation dialog appears.
10. Click **Buy**. The application is purchased.
11. Click **Downloads** on the left side of the screen. The Downloads screen appears, as shown in **Figure 12**. iTunes may ask whether you want the program to check automatically whether you have downloads available. Click **Yes**. This will allow you to download any applications you may have bought but failed to download.
12. Click iPhone under 'Devices' when the download is finished. The iPhone summary screen appears.
13. Click **Sync** in the lower right-hand corner of the screen. The iPhone lights up and "Sync in Progress" appears at the top of the screen. The current task is displayed at the top of the screen. When "OK to disconnect" appears at the top of the screen, your new application is installed and you may unplug the iPhone from your computer.

Figure 10: iTunes Store on a Computer

Figure 11: Application Description

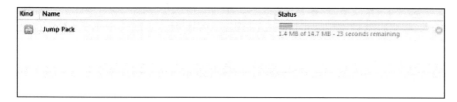

Figure 12: Downloads Screen

7. Using Wi-Fi to Download an Application

Applications that are over 10MB in size require the iPhone to be connected to a Wi-Fi network to download. These applications will display the following message: "Application over 10MB. Connect to a Wi-Fi network or use iTunes on your computer to download >APP NAME<", where APP NAME refers to the name of the application you are trying to download. Refer to *"Using Wi-Fi"* on page 29 to learn how to turn on Wi-Fi or to *"Using iTunes to Download an Application from a Computer"* on page 191 to learn how to use iTunes on your computer.

8. Switching Between Applications

The iPhone allows you to switch between running applications without having to exit any of them. For instance, you can listen to Pandora radio and read an eBook at the same time. To switch between running applications:

1. Touch an application icon on one of your Home screens. The application opens.
2. Press the **Home** button. The Home screen is shown.
3. Open another application. Press the Home button twice quickly. All of the open applications are displayed at the bottom of the screen, as shown in **Figure 13**.
4. Touch an application icon. The iPhone switches to the selected application.

Note: When switching to another application, the first application is never automatically closed. The application is simply running in the background. Refer to "Closing an Application Running in the Background" *on page 196 to learn how to close an application.*

Figure 13: Open Applications

9. Closing an Application Running in the Background

After pressing the Home button to exit an application, it is not closed, but is left running in the background instead. It is good to have the application running, because you can always switch to it quickly. However, if an application stops responding or if your battery is dying too quickly, you may wish to close it. To close an application that is running in the background:

1. Press the **Home** button twice quickly. All of the open applications are displayed at the bottom of the screen.
2. Touch and hold an application icon. The application icons at the bottom of the screen begin to shake.
3. Touch the ⊖ button next to an application icon. The application is closed.

10. Organizing Applications into Folders

To learn how to organize applications into folders, refer to *"Creating an Icon Folder"* on page 27.

11. Reading User Reviews

In order to make a more informed decision when purchasing an application, you can read the reviews written by other users. However, be aware that people who have not used the application can also post reviews, which are uninformed. To read user reviews for an application:

1. Touch the [icon] icon. The Application Store opens.
2. Find the application you want. Refer to *"Searching for an Application"* on page 186 to learn how.
3. Touch an application icon. The Application description appears.
4. Touch **Reviews** at the top of the screen. The Reviews screen appears, showing the first ten reviews.
5. Touch the screen and move your finger up to scroll to the bottom of the list. Touch **More Reviews** to read additional reviews.

12. Changing Application Settings

Some applications have settings that can be changed from the Settings screen. To change the Application settings, touch the [icon] icon. The Settings screen appears. Touch an application below 'Store' at the bottom of the screen. The Application Settings screen appears. The settings on this screen depend on the particular application.

13. Deleting an Application

You may delete most applications from your iPhone to free up space on your memory card or Home screen. To delete an unwanted application:

1. Touch and hold an application icon. All of the applications on the Home screen begin to shake. Applications that can be erased have an [×] button in their top left-hand corner.
2. Touch the [×] button next to an application icon. A confirmation dialog appears.
3. Touch **Delete**. The application is deleted.

4. Press the **Home** button. The application icons stop shaking and the ⊗ buttons disappear.

Note: If you delete a paid application, you can download it again free of charge at any time. Refer to "Buying an Application" on page 190 and follow the instructions for buying the application to re-download it through iTunes.

14. Redeeming a Gifted Application

Applications may be gifted through the iTuens store on your computer. When receiving an application as a gift, you must redeem it in order to download it. To redeem a gift and download the application using your iPhone:

1. Touch the [icon] icon. The email application opens.

2. Touch the email with the subject '**NAME sent you an iTunes Gift**', where NAME represents the name of the sender. The email opens. Refer to *"Reading Email"* on page 163 to learn how to find an email.

3. Touch the **Redeem Now** button in the email. The Application Store opens and the password prompt appears. Enter your iTunes password and touch **OK**. The gifted application is downloaded. If the application is over 10MB, you must first turn on Wi-Fi. Refer to *"Using Wi-Fi"* to learn how to turn Wi-Fi on.

15. Downloading FREE Applications from Your Computer

There are many free applications available for download through iTunes. To download a free application:

1. Install iTunes. Go to **www.itunes.com/download** to download it. Click **Download Now** and follow the on-screen instructions. Open iTunes.
2. Click **iTunes Store** on the left side of the screen. The iTunes Store home page appears.
3. Click **App Store** at the top of the page. The Application Store page appears.
4. Click **See All** under 'Free Apps'. The top free applications appear, as shown in **Figure 14**.
5. Click the **Get App** button next to an application you want. The password prompt appears.
6. Enter your iTunes password and click **Get**. The application is downloaded.

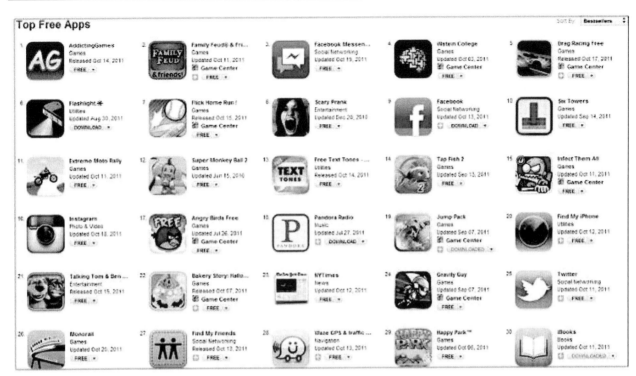

Figure 14: Top Free Applications

Using Siri

Siri is a voice-activated assistant that comes with the iPhone 5. Follow the tips in this chapter to use Siri to its full potential.

Table of Contents

1. Making a Call

To make a call using Siri, press and hold the **Home** button or hold the phone up to your ear and wait for Siri to speak. Say one of the following phrases:

- **Call John** (use any name)
- **Call Suzy Mobile**
- **Call Dexter on his work phone**
- **Call 123 555 1345**
- **Call home**
- **FaceTime Jacob**

Note: These phrases are only suggestions. Siri is flexible, and you can use many synonymous phrases.

2. Sending and Receiving Text Messages

To send, read, or reply to a text message using Siri, press and hold the **Home** button or hold the phone up to your ear and wait for Siri to speak. Say one of the following phrases:

- **Tell Anne See you soon**
- **Send a message to Rob Burr**
- **Send a message to Larry saying What's your address?**
- **Send a message to Julie on her mobile saying I got an iPhone 5!**
- **Send a message to 999 555 2222**
- **Text Jude and Prudence What are you guys up to today?**
- **Read my new messages**
- **Read it again**
- **Reply that's great news**
- **Tell him ETA is 20 minutes**
- **Call her**

Note: These phrases are only suggestions. Siri is flexible, and you can use many synonymous phrases.

3. Managing the Address Book

To manage the address book using Siri, press and hold the Home button or hold the phone up to your ear and wait for Siri to speak. Say one of the following phrases:

- **What's Joe's address?**
- **What is Susan Park's phone number?**
- **When is my grandfather's birthday?**
- **Show Bobby's email address**
- **Show Pete Abred**
- **Find people named Apple**
- **My brother is Trudy Ages** (assigns a relationship to the name)
- **Who is Colin Card?** (gives Colin Card's contact information)
- **Call my brother at home** (calls the number assigned to the relationship 'brother')

Note: These phrases are only suggestions. Siri is flexible, and you can use many synonymous phrases.

4. Setting Up and Managing Meetings

To set up and manage meetings using Siri, press and hold the **Home** button or hold the phone up to your ear and wait for Siri to speak. Say one of the following phrases:

- **Set up a meeting at 10**
- **Set up a meeting with Zoe at 9**
- **Meet with Nikki at noon**
- **New appointment with Dan Delion Tuesday at 4**
- **Schedule a focus group meeting at 3:30 today in the boardroom**
- **Move my 2pm meeting to 3:30**
- **Add Wendy to my meeting with Waldo**
- **Cancel the focus group meeting**
- **What does the rest of my day look like?**
- **What's on my calendar for Monday?**
- **When is my next appointment?**
- **Where is my next meeting?**

Note: These phrases are only suggestions. Siri is flexible, and you can use many synonymous phrases.

5. Checking the Time and Setting Alarms

To check the time and set alarms using Siri, press and hold the **Home** button or hold the phone up to your ear and wait for Siri to speak. Say one of the following phrases:

- **Wake me up tomorrow at 6am**
- **Set an alarm for 6:30am**
- **Wake me up in 8 hours**
- **Change my 5:30 alarm to 6:30**
- **Turn off my 4:30 alarm**
- **What time is it?**
- **What time is it in Moscow?**
- **What is today's date?**
- **What's the date this Friday?**
- **Set the timer for 30 minutes**
- **Show the timer**
- **Pause the timer**
- **Resume**
- **Reset the timer**
- **Stop the timer**

Note: These phrases are only suggestions. Siri is flexible, and you can use many synonymous phrases.

6. Sending and Receiving Email

To send and receive email using Siri, press and hold the **Home** button or hold the phone up to your ear and wait for Siri to speak. Say one of the following phrases:

- **Email Dave about the trip**
- **Email New email to John Diss**
- **Mail Dad about dinner**
- **Email Dr. Spaulding and say Got your message**
- **Mail Jack and Jill about the party and say It was awesome**
- **Check email**

Note: These phrases are only suggestions. Siri is flexible, and you can use many synonymous phrases.

7. Searching the Web and Asking Questions

To search the Web using Siri, press and hold the **Home** button or hold the phone up to your ear and wait for Siri to speak. Say one of the following phrases:

- **Search the web for Apple News**
- **Search for chili recipes**
- **Google the humane society**
- **Search Wikipedia for Duckbilled Platypus**
- **Bing Secondhand Serenade**
- **How many calories in a doughnut?**
- **What is an 18% tip on $180.45 for six people?**
- **How long do cats live?**
- **What's 25 squared?**
- **How many dollars is 60 euros?**
- **How many days until Christmas?**
- **When is the next solar eclipse?**
- **Show me the Ursula Major constellation**
- **What is the meaning of life?**
- **What's the price of gasoline in Boston?**

Note: These phrases are only suggestions. Siri is flexible, and you can use many synonymous phrases.

8. Looking Up Words in the Dictionary

To look up words using Siri, press and hold the **Home** button or hold the phone up to your ear and wait for Siri to speak. Say one of the following phrases:

- **What is the meaning of meticulous?**
- **Define albeit**
- **Look up the word jargon**

Note: These phrases are only suggestions. Siri is flexible, and you can use many phrases synonymous with these suggestions.

Adjusting the Settings

Table of Contents

Adjusting Wireless Settings

Table of Contents

1. Turning Airplane Mode On or Off

Most airplanes do not allow wireless communications while in flight. Continue using the iPhone while you fly by enabling Airplane mode before take-off. You may not place or receive calls, send or receive text messages or emails, or surf the Web while in Airplane mode. Airplane Mode is also useful when traveling outside of your area of service to avoid any roaming charges and to preserve battery life. To turn Airplane Mode on or off:

1. Touch the ![icon] icon. The Settings screen appears, as shown in **Figure 1**.
2. Touch the OFF switch next to 'Airplane Mode'. The ON switch appears and Airplane mode is turned on.
3. Touch the ON switch next to 'Airplane Mode'. The OFF switch appears and Airplane mode is turned off.

Figure 1: Settings Screen

2. Turning Location Services On or Off

Some iPhone applications require the Location Services feature to be turned on, which determines your current location. To turn Location Services on or off:

1. Touch the ![icon] icon. The Settings screen appears.
2. Touch **Privacy**. The Privacy Settings screen appears, as shown in **Figure 2**.
3. Touch **Location Services** at the top of the screen. The Location Services screen appears.
4. Touch the OFF switch next to 'Location Services'. The ON switch appears and Location Services are turned on.
5. Touch the ON switch next to 'Location Services'. The OFF switch appears and Location Services are turned off.

Figure 2: Privacy Settings Screen

3. Turning Data Roaming On or Off

When you are in an area with no wireless coverage, the iPhone can use the Data Roaming feature to acquire signal from other networks. Be aware that Data Roaming can be extremely costly. Contact your network provider for details. To turn Data Roaming on or off:

1. Touch the ![icon] icon. The Settings screen appears.
2. Touch **General**. The General Settings screen appears.
3. Touch **Cellular**. The Cellular Settings screen appears, as shown in **Figure 3**.
4. Touch the `OFF` switch next to 'Data Roaming'. The `ON` switch appears and Data Roaming is turned on.
5. Touch the `ON` switch next to 'Data Roaming'. The `OFF` switch appears and Data Roaming is turned off.

Figure 3: Cellular Settings Screen

4. Setting Up a Virtual Private Network (VPN)

You can use your iPhone to connect to an external network, such as a corporate one. To set up a VPN:

1. Touch the ![icon] icon. The Settings screen appears.
2. Touch **General**. The General Settings screen appears.
3. Touch **VPN**. The VPN screen appears, as shown in **Figure 4**.

4. Touch the ![OFF] switch next to 'VPN'. The Add Configuration screen appears, as shown in **Figure 5**.

5. Touch each field and enter the required information. Touch the ![Save] button in the upper right-hand corner of the screen when you are finished. The VPN is set up.

Figure 4: VPN Screen

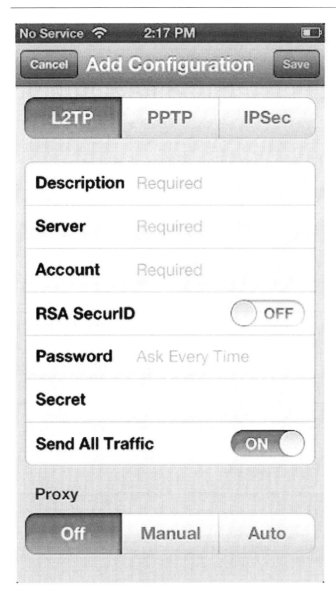

Figure 5: Add Configuration Screen

5. Turning Bluetooth On or Off

A wireless Bluetooth headset can be used with the iPhone. Be aware that leaving Bluetooth turned on while the headset is not in use consumes up a lot of battery life. To turn Bluetooth on or off:

1. Touch the [icon] icon. The Settings screen appears.
2. Touch **General**. The General Settings screen appears.
3. Touch **Bluetooth**. The Bluetooth Settings screen appears, as shown in **Figure 6**.
4. Touch the OFF switch on the right-hand side of the screen. Bluetooth is turned on and a list of devices appears. If there are no Bluetooth devices near the iPhone, the list will be empty.
5. Touch the ON switch. Bluetooth is turned off.

Figure 6: Bluetooth Settings Screen

Adjusting Sound Settings

Table of Contents

1. Turning Vibration On or Off

The iPhone can be set to vibrate every time it rings or only while it is in Silent Mode. To turn Ringer Vibration on or off:

1. Touch the ![icon] icon. The Settings screen appears, as shown in **Figure 1**.
2. Touch **Sounds**. The Sound Settings screen appears, as shown in **Figure 2**.
3. Touch the OFF switch next to 'Vibrate on Ring' under the 'Vibrate' section. The ON switch appears and Ringer Vibration is turned on. The iPhone will vibrate whenever there is an incoming call.
4. Touch the ON switch. The OFF switch appears, Ringer Vibration is turned off, and the iPhone will not vibrate for incoming calls.

To turn Silent Mode vibration on or off:

1. Touch the ![icon] icon. The Settings screen appears.
2. Touch **Sounds**. The Sound Settings screen appears.
3. Touch the OFF switch next to 'Vibrate on Silent' under the 'Vibrate' section. The ON switch appears and Silent Mode vibration is turned on. The iPhone will vibrate whenever a call or message is received in Silent Mode.
4. Touch the ON switch. The OFF switch appears, and Silent Mode Vibration is turned off. The iPhone will not vibrate when it is in Silent Mode.

Note: To turn on Silent Mode on the iPhone, put the vibration switch in the down position so that a red line appears above it. Silent mode is turned on. Refer to "Button Layout" on page 11 to view the location of the Vibration switch.

Figure 1: Settings Screen

Figure 2: Sound Settings Screen

2. Turning Volume Button Functionality On or Off

The volume buttons can be used to adjust the volume of the media, alerts, and the ringer. When the volume button functionality is disabled, they no longer work. To turn the volume button functionality on or off:

1. Touch the [icon] icon. The Settings screen appears.
2. Touch **Sounds**. The Sound Settings screen appears.
3. Touch the [ON] switch next to 'Change with Buttons' under the 'Ringer and Alerts' section. The [OFF] switch appears and volume button functionality is turned off.
4. Touch the [OFF] switch next to 'Change with Buttons'. The [ON] switch appears and the volume button functionality is turned on.

3. Setting the Default Ringtone

You may change the ringtone that sounds every time somebody calls you. To set a default ringtone:

1. Touch the [icon] icon. The Settings screen appears.
2. Touch **Sounds**. The Sound Settings screen appears.
3. Touch **Ringtone** under the 'Ringer and Alerts' section. A list of ringtones appears, as shown in **Figure 3**.
4. Touch a ringtone. The new default ringtone is selected and a preview plays.

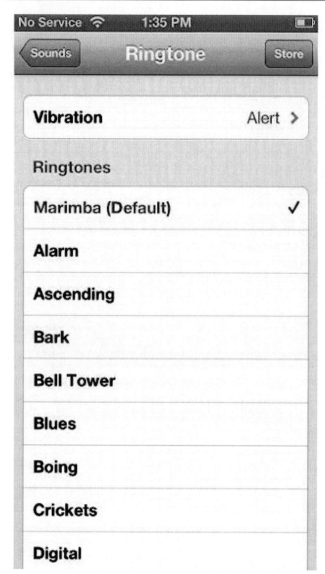

Figure 3: List of Ringtones

4. Customizing Notification and Alert Sounds

There are several notification and alert sounds that can be changed on the iPhone. To customize notification and alert sounds:

1. Touch the ![icon] icon. The Settings screen appears.
2. Touch **Sounds**. The Sound Settings screen appears.
3. Touch one of the following options under the 'Ringer and Alerts' section to change the corresponding sound:

   - **Text Tone** - Plays when a new text message arrives.
   - **New Voicemail** - Plays when a new voicemail arrives.
   - **New Mail** - Plays when a new email arrives.
   - **Sent Mail** - Plays when an email is sent from the iPhone.
   - **Tweet** - Plays when a new Tweet arrives.
   - **Facebook Post** - Plays when a new Facebook notification arrives.
   - **Calendar Alerts** - Plays as a reminder for a calendar event.
   - **Reminder Alerts** - Plays as a notification of a previously set reminder.

5. Turning Lock Sounds On or Off

The iPhone can make a sound every time it is locked or unlocked. By default, this sound is turned on. To turn Lock Sounds on or off:

1. Touch the ![icon] icon. The Settings screen appears.
2. Touch **Sounds**. The Sound Settings screen appears.
3. Scroll down and touch the ![ON switch] switch next to 'Lock Sounds' at the bottom of the screen. The ![OFF switch] switch appears and Lock sounds are turned off.
4. Touch the ![OFF switch] switch next to 'Lock Sounds' at the bottom of the screen. The ![ON switch] switch appears and Lock sounds are turned on.

6. Turning Keyboard Clicks On or Off

The iPhone can make a sound every time a key is touched on the virtual keyboard. By default, Keyboard Clicks are turned on. To turn Keyboard Clicks on or off:

1. Touch the ![icon] icon. The Settings screen appears.
2. Touch **Sounds**. The Sound Settings screen appears.
3. Scroll down and touch the ON switch next to 'Keyboard Clicks' at the bottom of the screen. The OFF switch appears and Keyboard Clicks are turned off.
4. Touch the OFF switch next to 'Keyboard Clicks' at the bottom of the screen. The ON switch appears and Keyboard Clicks are turned on.

Adjusting Language and Keyboard Settings

Table of Contents

1. Customizing Spelling and Grammar Settings

Customize the Spelling and Grammar settings on your iPhone to improve typing accuracy when composing text messages or emails. To customize the Spelling and Grammar settings:

1. Touch the 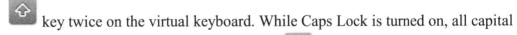 icon. The Settings screen appears, as shown in **Figure 1**.
2. Touch **General**. The General Settings screen appears, as shown in **Figure 2**.
3. Touch **Keyboard**. The Keyboard Settings screen appears, as shown in **Figure 3**.
4. Touch one of the following switches on the right-hand side of the screen to turn the corresponding setting on or off:

   - **Auto-Capitalization** - Capitalizes the first word of every sentence automatically.
   - **Auto-Correction** - Suggests and makes text corrections while you type.
   - **Check Spelling** - Underlines all misspelled words.
   - **Enable Caps Lock** - Allows you to turn Caps Lock on by quickly touching the

     ⬆ key twice on the virtual keyboard. While Caps Lock is turned on, all capital

     letters are typed without the need to use the ⬆ key.
   - **"." Shortcut** – Allows a period and an extra space to be inserted when you quickly touch the space bar twice.

Figure 1: Settings Screen

Figure 2: General Settings Screen

Figure 3: Keyboard Settings Screen

2. Adding an International Keyboard

The iPhone allows you to use international keyboards when entering text on the virtual keyboard. To add an international keyboard:

1. Touch the  icon. The Settings screen appears.
2. Touch **General**. The General Settings screen appears.
3. Touch **Keyboard**. The Keyboard Settings screen appears.
4. Touch **Keyboards**. The Keyboards screen appears, as shown in **Figure 4**.
5. Touch **Add New Keyboard**. A list of international keyboards appears, as shown in **Figure 5**.
6. Touch a keyboard. The keyboard is added and appears on the Keyboards screen. While typing, touch the key at the bottom of the virtual keyboard to switch to an international one.

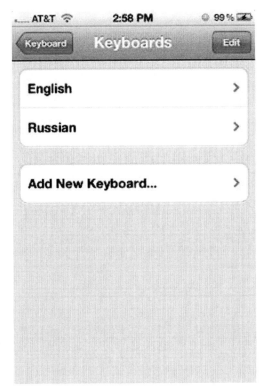

Figure 4: Keyboards Screen

Figure 5: List of International Keyboards

3. Adding a Keyboard Shortcut

The iPhone allows you to add custom Keyboard shortcuts. For example, "ur" for "your" or "ttyl" for "talk to you later" are substituted when the corresponding abbreviation is typed. To add a Keyboard shortcut:

1. Touch the ![icon] icon. The Settings screen appears.
2. Touch **General**. The General Settings screen appears.
3. Touch **Keyboard**. The Keyboard Settings screen appears.
4. Touch **Add New Shortcut** at the bottom of the screen. The Shortcut screen appears, as shown in **Figure 6**.
5. Type the desired phrase to be substituted for the shortcut. Touch **return**.

6. Type the desired shortcut and touch the ![Save] button in the upper right-hand corner of the screen. The keyboard shortcut is added. To use the shortcut, type it and touch the space bar.

Figure 6: Shortcut Screen

4. Changing the Operating System Language

The iOS on the iPhone can be changed to display all menus and options in a language other than English. To change the Operating System Language:

1. Touch the ![icon] icon. The Settings screen appears.
2. Touch **General**. The General Settings screen appears.
3. Touch **International**. The International screen appears, as shown in **Figure 7**.
4. Touch **Language**. A list of available languages appears, as shown in **Figure 8**.
5. Touch a language and touch the **Done** button in the upper right-hand corner of the screen. The selected language is applied and all menus and options reflect the change.

Figure 7: International Screen

Figure 8: List of Available Languages

5. Changing the Voice Control Language

You can change the required input language for the Voice Control feature. To change the Voice Control language:

1. Touch the  icon. The Settings screen appears.
2. Touch **General**. The General Settings screen appears.
3. Touch **International**. The International screen appears.
4. Touch **Voice Control**. A list of languages appears.
5. Touch a language. The selected language will be used for Voice Control input.

Note: Press and hold the Home button to activate Voice Control. The Voice Control screen appears, as shown in **Figure 9**.

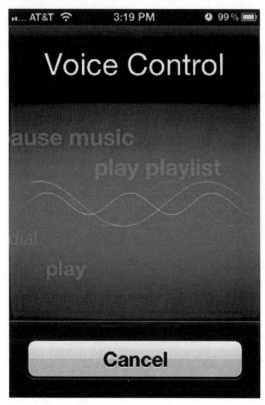

Figure 9: Voice Control Screen

6. Changing the Keyboard Layout

The layout of the keyboard in most languages can be changed, according to personal preference. For instance, the English keyboard can be set display in default QWERTY, as shown in **Figure 10**, AZERTY, as shown in **Figure 11**, or QWERTZ as shown in **Figure 12**. To change the Keyboard Layout:

1. Touch the icon. The Settings screen appears.
2. Touch **General**. The General Settings screen appears.
3. Touch **Keyboard**. The Keyboard Settings screen appears.
4. Touch **International Keyboards**. The Keyboards screen appears.
5. Touch the language of the keyboard that you wish to change. The Keyboard Layout screen appears.
6. Touch the desired layout. The new Keyboard Layout is set.

Figure 10: QWERTY Keyboard

Figure 11: AZERTY Keyboard

Figure 12: QWERTZ Keyboard

7. Changing the Region Format

The region format on the iPhone determines how dates, times, and phone numbers are universally displayed. For instance, a European country may display the 30th day of the first month in the year 2011 as 30/01/2011, whereas the U.S. would display the same date as 01/30/2011. To change the region format:

1. Touch the  icon. The Settings screen appears.
2. Touch **General**. The General Settings screen appears.
3. Touch **International**. The International screen appears.
4. Touch **Region Format**. A list of region formats appears, as shown in **Figure 13**.
5. Touch the desired format. The new format is set.

Figure 13: List of Region Formats

Adjusting General Settings

Table of Contents

1. Changing Auto-Lock Settings

The iPhone can lock itself when it is idle in order to save battery life and to avoid unintentionally pressing buttons. When it is locked, the iPhone can still receive calls and text messages. By default, the iPhone is set to automatically lock after one minute. To change the length of time that will pass before the iPhone locks itself:

1. Touch the icon. The Settings screen appears, as shown in **Figure 1**.
2. Touch **General**. The General Settings screen appears, as shown in **Figure 2**.
3. Touch **Auto-Lock**. The Auto-Lock Settings screen appears, as shown in **Figure 3**.
4. Touch an amount of time, or touch **Never** if you do not want the iPhone to automatically lock itself. The change is applied and the iPhone will wait the selected amount of time before automatically locking itself.

Figure 1: Settings Screen

Figure 2: General Settings Screen

Figure 3: Auto-Lock Settings Screen

2. Adjusting the Brightness

You may wish to increase the brightness of the screen on your iPhone when you are in a sunny area. On the other hand, you may wish to decrease the brightness in a dark area to conserve battery life and rest your eyes. You can also turn Auto-Brightness on or off, which will determine whether or not the iPhone automatically sets the brightness based on the lighting conditions. To adjust the brightness:

1. Touch the icon. The Settings screen appears.
2. Touch **Brightness & Wallpaper**. The Brightness & Wallpaper Settings screen appears, as shown in **Figure 4**.
3. Touch the on the bar and drag it towards the small icon to decrease the brightness or towards the large icon to increase it.
4. Touch the switch next to 'Auto-Brightness' to disable Auto-Brightness or touch the switch to enable it. Auto-Brightness is turned disabled or enabled.

Note: While Auto-Brightness is enabled, you can still temporarily adjust the brightness of the screen. However, as soon as the lighting conditions change, the iPhone will automatically change the brightness accordingly.

Figure 4: Brightness & Wallpaper Settings Screen

3. Assigning a Passcode Lock

The iPhone can prompt for either a four-digit or an alphanumeric password before unlocking. To set or change the password:

1. Touch the ![icon] icon. The Settings screen appears.
2. Touch **General**. The General Settings screen appears.
3. Scroll down and touch Passcode Lock. The Passcode Lock screen appears, as shown in **Figure 5**.
4. Touch **Turn Passcode On**. The Set Passcode screen appears, as shown in **Figure 6**, if the Simple Passcode feature is turned on. The Set Password screen appears, as shown in **Figure 7**, if the Simple Passcode feature is turned off.
5. Type a passcode. A confirmation screen appears.
6. Type the passcode again. The new passcode is set.
7. Touch one of the following options on the Passcode Lock screen to change the corresponding setting:
    *   **Require Passcode** – Set the time the iPhone waits before asking the user for the passcode. It is recommended to choose the default, Immediately, since an unauthorized user will not have access to your iPhone for any period of time if this option is chosen. Choosing one of the other options causes the iPhone to wait a set amount of time after becoming active before requiring a passcode.
    *   **Simple Passcode** – Allows you to enter a four-digit passcode. When turned off, you must enter an alphanumeric password when setting the passcode.
    *   **Erase Data** – Erases all data after a user enters the passcode incorrectly ten times in a row. *Warning: You will not be able to recover your data if this feature is on when an incorrect passcode is entered ten times consecutively.*

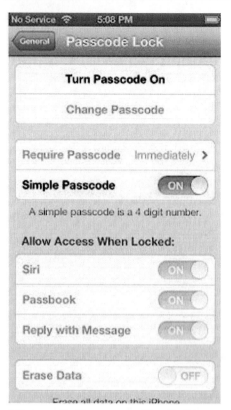

Figure 5: Passcode Lock Screen

Figure 6: Set Passcode Screen

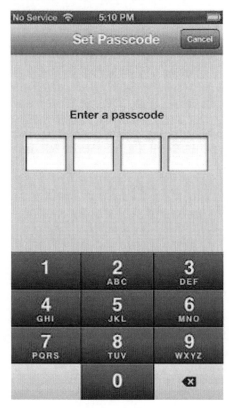

Figure 7: Set Password Screen

4. Changing a Passcode Lock

After setting up a Passcode lock, you may change its settings. To change a Passcode lock:

1. Touch the ![icon] icon. The Settings screen appears.
2. Touch **General**. The General Settings screen appears.
3. Touch **Passcode Lock**. The Passcode Lock screen appears.
4. Touch **Change Passcode**. The Change Passcode screen appears, as shown in **Figure 8**.
5. Enter your old passcode, then enter a new passcode twice. The passcode is changed.

Figure 8: Change Passcode Screen

5. Turning Off the Passcode Lock

While using a passcode will keep your iPhone more secure, it will also take longer to unlock the iPhone. To turn off the Passcode lock:

1. Touch the ![icon] icon. The Settings screen appears.
2. Touch **General**. The General Settings screen appears.
3. Touch **Passcode Lock**. The Passcode Lock screen appears.
4. Touch **Turn Passcode Off**. The iPhone requests your passcode.
5. Enter your current passcode. The passcode is turned off.
6.

6. Turning 24-Hour Mode On or Off

The iPhone can display the time in regular 12-hour mode or in 24-hour mode, commonly referred to as military time. To turn 24-hour mode on or off:

1. Touch the ![icon] icon. The Settings screen appears.
2. Touch **General**. The General Settings screen appears.
3. Touch **Date & Time**. The Date & Time screen appears, as shown in **Figure 9**.
4. Touch the OFF switch next to '24-Hour Time. The ON switch appears and 24-Hour mode is turned on.
5. Touch the ON switch next to '24-Hour Time. The OFF switch appears and 24-Hour mode is turned off.

Figure 9: Date & Time Screen

7. Resetting the Home Screen Layout

You can reset the Home screen on your iPhone to look like it did when you first purchased it. To reset the Home Screen Layout:

Note: Resetting the Home screen layout does not delete any applications, but simply rearranges them.

1. Touch the ![settings icon] icon. The Settings screen appears.
2. Touch **General**. The General Settings screen appears.
3. Touch **Reset** at the bottom of the screen. The Reset screen appears, as shown in **Figure 10**.
4. Touch **Reset Home Screen Layout**. A confirmation appears at the bottom of the screen.
5. Touch the ![Reset Home Screen button] button. The Home Screen Layout is reset.

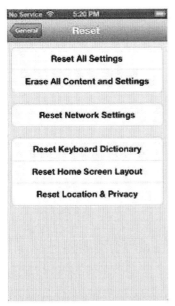

Figure 10: Reset Screen

8. Resetting All Settings

You can reset all of the settings on your iPhone to the state they were in when you first purchased it. To reset all settings:

Note: Resetting the settings will NOT delete any data from your iPhone.

1. Touch the ![icon] icon. The Settings screen appears.
2. Touch **General**. The General Settings screen appears.
3. Touch **Reset**. The Reset screen appears.
4. Touch **Reset All Settings**. A confirmation appears at the bottom of the screen.
5. Touch the **Reset All Settings** button. All settings are reset to defaults.

9. Erasing and Restoring the iPhone

You can delete all of the data and reset all settings to completely restore the iPhone to its original condition. To erase and restore the iPhone to its original condition:

Warning: Any erased data is not recoverable. Make sure you back up all of the data you wish to keep.

1. Touch the ![icon] icon. The Settings screen appears.
2. Touch **General**. The General Settings screen appears.
3. Touch **Reset** at the bottom of the screen. The Reset screen appears.
4. Touch **Erase All Content and Settings**. A confirmation appears at the bottom of the screen.
5. Touch the **Erase iPhone** button. Data on the iPhone is erased, and the iPhone is restored to its original condition.

Adjusting Accessibility Settings

Table of Contents

1. Turning VoiceOver On or Off

VoiceOver is a feature designed for visually impaired iPhone users and for those who wish to listen to their eBooks in the Kindle and iBooks applications. VoiceOver pronounces everything that is on the screen, including letters and characters that are typed. To turn VoiceOver on or off:

1. Touch the ![icon] icon. The Settings screen appears, as shown in **Figure 1**.
2. Touch **General**. The General Settings screen appears, as shown in **Figure 2**.
3. Scroll down and touch **Accessibility**. The Accessibility Settings screen appears, as shown in **Figure 3**.
4. Touch **Voiceover** under the 'Vision' section. The Voiceover Settings screen appears, as shown in **Figure 4**.
5. Touch the ![OFF] switch next to 'VoiceOver'. The ![ON] switch appears and VoiceOver is turned on.
6. Touch the ![ON] switch next to 'VoiceOver'. The ![OFF] switch appears and VoiceOver is turned off.

Note: While Voiceover is activated, you must touch each item once to have it spoken out loud and twice to select it. You must touch the screen with three fingers to scroll through a list.

Figure 1: Settings Screen

Figure 2: General Settings Screen

Figure 3: Accessibility Settings Screen

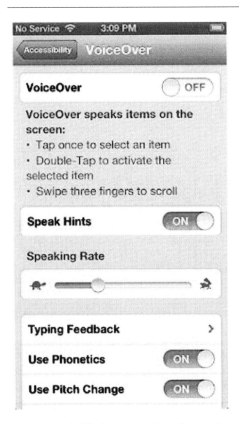

Figure 4: Voiceover Settings Screen

2. Turning Zoom On or Off

Zoom is a feature that allows you to magnify any part of the screen. To turn Zoom on or off:

1. Touch the ![icon] icon. The Settings screen appears.
2. Touch **General**. The General Settings screen appears.
3. Scroll down and touch **Accessibility**. The Accessibility Settings screen appears.
4. Touch **Zoom** under the 'Vision' section. The Zoom screen appears, as shown in **Figure 5**.
5. Touch the ![OFF] switch next to 'Zoom'. The ![ON] switch appears, the iPhone zooms in, and Zoom is turned on.
6. Touch the ![ON] switch next to 'Zoom'. The ![OFF] switch appears and Zoom is turned off.
7. Use the following tips to use the Zoom feature:
    *   Quickly touch the screen twice using three fingers to zoom in.
    *   Quickly touch the screen twice using three fingers and then, without releasing the screen, drag up to increase the zoom level or down to decrease it.
    *   Touch the screen with three fingers and drag in any direction to move around the screen while zoomed in.

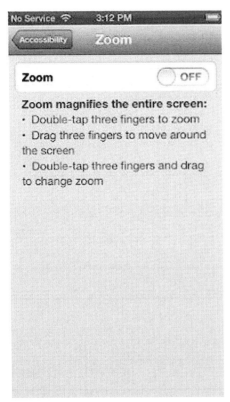

Figure 5: Zoom Screen

3. Turning Large Text On or Off

You can customize the size of the text in the calendar, contacts, email, text messages, or notes by changing one setting, called Large Text. To turn Large Text on or off:

1. Touch the icon. The Settings screen appears.
2. Touch **General**. The General Settings screen appears.
3. Scroll down and touch **Accessibility**. The Accessibility Settings screen appears.
4. Touch **Large Text** under the 'Vision' section. The Large Text screen appears, as shown in **Figure 6**.
5. Touch a text size, each of which is shown as it will appear on the screen. Large Text is turned on and the new text size is applied.

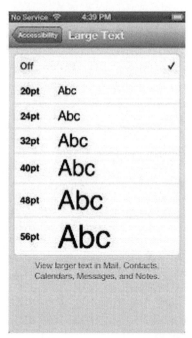

Figure 6: Large Text Screen

4. Inverting the Color Scheme

For individuals who have difficulty looking at backlit screens for long periods of time, the iPhone allows you to invert all colors on the screen. To invert the color scheme:

1. Touch the icon. The Settings screen appears.
2. Touch **General**. The General Settings screen appears.
3. Touch **Accessibility**. The Accessibility Settings screen appears.
4. Touch the OFF switch next to 'Invert Colors' under the 'Vision' section. The ON switch appears and the colors are inverted.
5. Touch the ON switch next to 'Invert Colors'. The OFF switch appears and the normal color scheme returns.

5. Turning Hearing Aid Mode On or Off

Hearing Aid mode is a feature for those who use hearing aids, and is specifically designed to reduce interference and feedback associated with putting a telephone next to a hearing aid. To turn Hearing Aid mode on or off:

1. Touch the ![icon] icon. The Settings screen appears.
2. Touch **General**. The General Settings screen appears.
3. Touch **Accessibility**. The Accessibility Settings screen appears.
4. Touch **Hearing Aids** under the 'Hearing' section. The Hearing Aids screen appears, as shown in **Figure 7**.
5. Touch the `OFF` switch next to 'Hearing Aid Mode' under the 'Hearing' section. The `ON` switch appears and Hearing Aid Mode is turned on.
6. Touch the `ON` switch next to 'Hearing Aid Mode'. The `OFF` switch appears and Hearing Aid Mode is turned off.

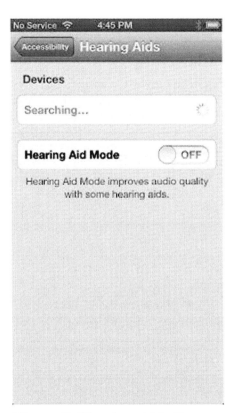

Figure 7: Hearing Aids Screen

6. Creating a New Vibration Pattern

In addition to selecting a pre-made vibration pattern, you can also create your own custom vibrations to use like custom ringtones. To create a new vibration pattern:

1. Touch the ![icon] icon. The Settings screen appears.
2. Touch **Sounds**. The Sound Settings screen appears.
3. Touch **Vibration**. The Vibration screen appears.
4. Touch **Create New Vibration**. The New Vibration screen appears, as shown in **Figure 8**.
5. Touch the screen quickly to create a short vibration or touch and hold it to create a long one. Keep touching the screen until the recording is complete.
6. Touch the ![▶ Play] button. The pattern you created plays. Touch the ![● Record] button to create a different pattern and repeat steps 1-5.
7. Touch the ![Save] button in the upper right-hand corner of the screen when you are satisfied with the pattern. The Vibration Name window appears.
8. Type a name for the new vibration and touch **Save**. The new vibration pattern is saved and appears on the Vibration screen above 'Create New Vibration'.

Figure 8: New Vibration Screen

7. Turning LED Flash Alerts On or Off

The iPhone can use the LED flash to notify you when there is an incoming text message. To turn LED flash alerts on or off:

1. Touch the icon. The Settings screen appears.
2. Touch **General**. The General Settings screen appears.
3. Scroll down and touch **Accessibility**. The Accessibility Settings screen appears.
4. Touch the ⬭ OFF switch next to 'LED Flash for Alerts' in the 'Hearing' section. The ON⬤ switch appears and LED Flash for Alerts is turned on.
5. Touch the ON⬤ switch next to 'LED Flash for Alerts'. The ⬭ OFF switch appears and LED Flash for Alerts is turned off.

8. Using the Speakerphone as a Default for Incoming Calls

You can set the iPhone to automatically turn on the speakerphone after answering a call. To use the speakerphone as the default for incoming calls:

1. Touch the ![icon] icon. The Settings screen appears.
2. Touch **General**. The General Settings screen appears.
3. Touch **Accessibility**. The Accessibility Settings screen appears.
4. Touch **Incoming calls**. The Incoming Calls screen appears, as shown in **Figure 9**.
5. Touch **Speaker**. The speakerphone will now be used by default for all incoming calls.

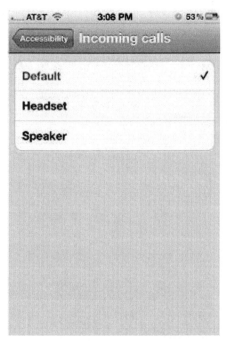

Figure 9: Incoming Calls Screen

9. Customizing the Triple-Click Home Shortcut

The Home button can be customized to perform an action when it is quickly pressed three times. This feature saves you from having to go through several menus to get to an Accessibility setting that you use often. To customize the Triple-Click Home shortcut:

1. Touch the ![icon] icon. The Settings screen appears.
2. Touch **General**. The General Settings screen appears.

3. Scroll down and touch **Accessibility**. The Accessibility Settings screen appears.
4. Touch **Triple-Click Home** under the 'Triple-Click' section at the bottom of the screen. The Triple-Click menu appears, as shown in **Figure 10**.
5. Touch an action to assign it to the Triple-Click Home shortcut. The action is assigned and a check mark appears next to the option.

*Note: Touch **Home-Click Speed** under the 'Physical & Motor' section on the Accessibility Settings screen in order to adjust the speed at which you need to press the Home button when activating the Triple-Click Home shortcut.*

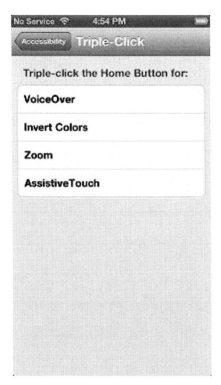

Figure 10: Triple-Click Menu

Adjusting Phone Settings

Table of Contents

1. Customizing the Text Message Replies Sent to Callers

During an incoming call, you may reject it and automatically send a text message to the caller. You may customize the text messages that are sent to the caller. To customize the text message replies sent to callers:

1. Touch the icon. The Settings screen appears, as shown in **Figure 1**.
2. Touch **Phone**. The Phone Settings screen appears, as shown in **Figure 2**.
3. Touch **Reply with Message**. The Reply with Message screen appears, as shown in **Figure 3**.
4. Touch one of the text fields under 'Can't talk right now…' and enter the desired reply. Touch **Phone** in the upper left-hand corner of the screen. The new text message reply is saved.

Figure 1: Settings Screen

Figure 2: Phone Settings Screen

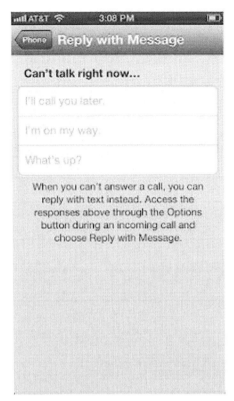

Figure 3: Reply with Message Screen

2. Turning Call Forwarding On or Off

The iPhone can be set to forward all calls to a specified number. To turn Call Forwarding on or off:

1. Touch the icon. The Settings screen appears.
2. Touch **Phone**. The Phone Settings screen appears.
3. Touch **Call Forwarding**. The Call Forwarding screen appears.
4. Touch the OFF switch next to 'Call Forwarding'. The 'Forward to' field appears, as shown in **Figure 4**.
5. Touch **Forward to**. The Forwarding To screen appears.
6. Use the keypad to enter the phone number to which the phone should forward. When finished, touch the Call Forwarding button in the upper left-hand corner of the screen. Call Forwarding is setup and the Call Forwarding screen appears.

Figure 4: Forwarding To Screen

3. Turning Call Waiting On or Off

While you are on the line with someone, the Call Waiting feature allows the iPhone to alert you when there is a second incoming call. To turn Call Waiting on or off:

1. Touch the ![icon] icon. The Settings screen appears.
2. Touch **Phone**. The Phone Settings screen appears.
3. Touch **Call Waiting**. The Call Waiting screen appears, as shown in **Figure 5**.
4. Touch the ON switch next to 'Call Waiting'. The OFF switch appears and Call Waiting is turned off.
5. Touch the OFF switch next to 'Call Waiting'. The ON switch appears and Call Waiting is turned on.

Figure 5: Call Waiting Screen

4. Turning Caller ID On or Off

The Caller ID feature shows your phone number or name (if your number is stored in the recipient's Phonebook) on the called party's device. In order to preserve privacy and make your phone number appear as "Private Number", turn the Caller ID feature off. To turn Caller ID on or off:

1. Touch the ![icon] icon. The Settings screen appears.
2. Touch **Phone**. The Phone Settings screen appears.
3. Touch **Show My Caller ID**. The Show My Caller ID screen appears, as shown in **Figure 6**.
4. Touch the ![ON] switch next to 'Show My Caller ID'. The ![OFF] switch appears and Caller ID is turned off.
5. Touch the ![OFF] switch next to 'Show My Caller ID'. The ![ON] switch appears and Caller ID is turned on.

Note: When Caller ID is turned off, even those who have your phone number stored in their Phonebook will not be able to view your number when receiving a call from you.

Figure 6: Show My Caller ID Screen

5. Turning TTY Mode On or Off

TTY stands for 'text telephone' or 'teletypewriter'. Using a special TTY machine when this mode is enabled allows speech and hearing impaired users to read incoming speech as text and type responses. The typed text is converted to speech on the other side of the conversation. Search Google for **TTY machine** to purchase one. You will also need an Apple TTY Adapter, which can be purchased here at the Apple Store, in order to plug in a TTY machine to the iPhone. To turn TTY Mode on or off:

1. Touch the [icon] icon. The Settings screen appears.
2. Touch **Phone**. The Phone Settings screen appears.
3. Touch the [OFF] switch next to 'TTY'. The [ON] switch appears and TTY mode is turned on.
4. Touch the [ON] switch next to 'TTY'. The [OFF] switch appears and TTY mode is turned off.

6. Turning the Dial Assist On or Off

The Dial Assist feature is useful while traveling abroad. This feature will automatically add the correct international prefix to every phone number you dial when calling a U.S. phone number. To turn Dial Assist on or off:

1. Touch the icon. The Settings screen appears.
2. Touch **Phone**. The Phone Settings screen appears.
3. Touch the switch next to 'Dial Assist'. The switch appears and Dial Assist is turned on.
4. Touch the switch next to 'Dial Assist'. The switch appears and Dial Assist is turned off.

Note: The Dial Assist feature does not work in all areas.

Adjusting Text Message Settings

Table of Contents

1. Turning iMessage On or Off

The iMessage feature allows you to send free text messages to another iPhone, iPad, or iPod Touch. Turn on iMessage to send a message to another iPhone or to an iPad or iPod touch using the email address assigned to the recipient's iMessage account. By default, iMessage is turned on. When iMessage is turned off and you send a text message to another device, standard text messaging rates apply as set forth by your network provider. To turn iMessage on or off:

1. Touch the icon. The Settings screen appears, as shown in **Figure 1**.
2. Touch **Messages**. The Message Settings screen appears, as shown in **Figure 2**.
3. Touch the OFF switch next to 'iMessage'. The ON switch appears and iMessage is turned on.
4. Touch the ON switch next to 'iMessage'. The OFF switch appears and iMessage is turned off.

Figure 1: Settings Screen

Figure 2: Message Settings Screen

2. Turning Read Receipts On or Off in iMessage

After receiving and opening a message from an iPhone, iPad, or iPod Touch, your iPhone can notify the sender that you have opened and read the message. These notifications are called Read Receipts, and appear under the original message on the sender's screen as "Read", followed by a time. By default, Read Receipts are only compatible with iPhones, iPads, and iPod Touches. To turn Read Receipts on or off:

1. Touch the ![icon] icon. The Settings screen appears.
2. Touch **Messages**. The Message Settings screen appears.
3. Touch the ![OFF] switch next to 'Send Read Receipts'. The ![ON] switch appears and Read Receipts are turned on.
4. Touch the ![ON] switch next to 'Send Read Receipts'. The ![OFF] switch appears and Read Receipts are turned off.

3. Turning 'Send as SMS' On or Off

When a message cannot be sent via iMessage, the iPhone can attempt to send it as a regular text message, or SMS. By default, Send as SMS is turned on. To turn Send as SMS on or off:

1. Touch the ![icon] icon. The Settings screen appears.
2. Touch **Messages**. The Message Settings screen appears.
3. Touch the `OFF` switch next to 'Send as SMS'. The `ON` switch appears and 'Send as SMS' is turned on.
4. Touch the `ON` switch next to 'Send as SMS'. The `OFF` switch appears and 'Send as SMS' is turned off.

Warning: When 'Send as SMS' is turned off, you will only be able to send a message to an iPhone, iPad, or iPod, which has iMessage enabled.

4. Turning MMS Messaging On or Off

When you are running low on data, it can be useful to disable MMS messaging in order to avoid receiving unwanted picture messages that will use up the data too quickly. To turn MMS messaging on or off:

1. Touch the ![icon] icon. The Settings screen appears.
2. Touch **Messages**. The Message Settings screen appears.
3. Touch the `ON` switch next to 'MMS Messaging' under 'SMS/MMS'. The `OFF` switch appears and MMS Messaging is turned off.
4. Touch the `OFF` switch next to 'MMS Messaging'. The `ON` switch appears and MMS Messaging is turned on.

5. Turning the Subject Field On or Off

The iPhone can attach a subject to each text message it sends when the subject field is enabled. On most phones, the subject will appear in parentheses preceding the message content. To turn the Subject field on or off:

1. Touch the [icon] icon. The Settings screen appears.
2. Touch **Messages**. The Message Settings screen appears.
3. Touch the [OFF] switch next to 'Show Subject Field'. The [ON] switch appears and the Subject field is turned on.
4. Touch the [ON] switch next to 'Show Subject Field'. The [OFF] switch appears and the Subject field is turned off.

6. Turning the Character Count On or Off

While typing a text message, the iPhone can display the number of characters that you have typed so far. To turn the Character Count on or off:

1. Touch the [icon] icon. The Settings screen appears.
2. Touch **Messages**. The Message Settings screen appears.
3. Touch the [OFF] switch next to 'Character Count'. The [ON] switch appears and Character Count is turned on.
4. Touch the [ON] switch next to 'Character Count'. The [OFF] switch appears and Character Count is turned off.

Adjusting Music Application Settings

Table of Contents

1. Turning 'Shake to Shuffle' On or Off

When the 'Shake to Shuffle' feature is enabled, the iPhone can shuffle the songs in the current playlist when you shake the phone. To turn 'Shake to Shuffle' on or off:

1. Touch the icon. The Settings screen appears, as shown in **Figure 1**.
2. Scroll down and touch Music. The Music Settings screen appears, as shown in **Figure 2**.
3. Touch the switch next to 'Shake to Shuffle'. The switch appears and 'Shake to Shuffle' is turned off.
4. Touch the switch next to 'Shake to Shuffle'. The switch appears and 'Shake to Shuffle' is turned on.

Figure 1: Settings Screen

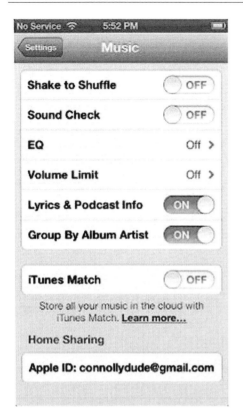

Figure 2: Music Settings Screen

2. Selecting a Pre-Loaded Equalization Setting

The iPhone has several custom, pre-loaded Equalization settings that can be applied in order to improve the sound of your music. To select an Equalization setting:

Note: In order to quickly select the optimal EQ setting for you, turn on some music before performing the steps below. Refer to "Using the Music Application" *on page 145 to learn how.*

1. Touch the ![icon] icon. The Settings screen appears.
2. Touch **Music**. The Music Settings screen appears.
3. Touch **EQ**. A list of EQ settings appears, as shown in **Figure 3**.
4. Touch an EQ setting. The EQ setting is applied to all music that plays via the Music application.

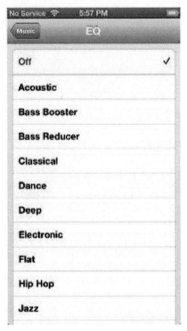

Figure 3: List of EQ Settings

3. Setting a Volume Limit

In order to prevent yourself from accidentally increasing the volume in the Music application when you accidentally press the volume buttons, try setting a Volume Limit. To set a Volume Limit:

1. Touch the icon. The Settings screen appears.
2. Touch **Music**. The Music Settings screen appears.
3. Touch **Volume Limit**. The Volume Limit screen appears, as shown in **Figure 4**.
4. Touch the on the bar and drag it to the desired location. The new volume limit is set.

4. Turning Lyrics and Podcast Info On or Off

The iPhone can automatically display the lyrics of a song or the details of a podcast while either of these is playing in the Music application. To turn 'Lyrics and Podcast Info' on or off:

1. Touch the ![icon] icon. The Settings screen appears.
2. Touch **Music**. The Music Settings screen appears.
3. Touch the OFF switch next to 'Lyrics & Podcast Info'. The ON switch appears and Lyrics and Podcast Info is turned on.
4. Touch the ON switch next to 'Lyrics & Podcast Info'. The OFF switch appears and Lyrics and Podcast Info is turned off.

Adjusting Photo and Video Settings

Table of Contents

1. Turning Photo Stream On or Off

Photo Stream allows you to instantly load photos that you have taken on your iPhone to your other registered Apple devices. It accomplishes this by automatically uploading them to the iCloud and then downloading them to the necessary devices. To turn Photo Stream on or off:

1. Touch the ![settings icon] icon. The Settings screen appears, as shown in **Figure 1**.
2. Scroll down and touch Photos + Camera. The Photos and Camera Settings screen appears, as shown in **Figure 2**.
3. Touch the OFF switch next to 'My Photo Stream'. The ON switch appears and Photo Stream is turned on. The iPhone may prompt you for your Apple ID and password before turning on Photo Stream.
4. Touch the ON switch next to 'My Photo Stream'. The OFF switch appears and Photo Stream is turned off.

Figure 1: Settings Screen

Figure 2: Photos and Camera Settings Screen

2. Customizing Slideshow Settings

You can customize the Slideshow settings on your iPhone. Refer to *"Starting a Slideshow"* on page 124 to learn how to turn on a slideshow. To customize Slideshow settings:

1. Touch the [icon] icon. The Settings screen appears.
2. Scroll down and touch **Photos + Camera**. The Photos and Camera Settings screen appears.
3. Touch one of the following options (or the On/Off switch) under the 'Slideshow' section to change the corresponding setting:

   - **Play Each Slide For** - Sets the amount of time each photo remains on the screen during a slideshow.
   - **Repeat** - Sets the slideshow to start again from the beginning of the current album after reaching the end.
   - **Shuffle** - Sets the photos to appear in random order during a slideshow. Note: Turning both 'Repeat' and 'Shuffle' on at the same time plays your photos continuously in random order.

3. Customizing High Dynamic Range (HDR) Camera Settings

When taking photos with the iPhone, you can enable HDR, which will improve picture quality by showing the lighting much more accurately than in a photo taken by a non-HDR camera. To turn on HDR, touch Options at the top of the screen while the camera is running and then touch the switch next to 'HDR'. When HDR is turned on, a non-HDR copy of each photo is stored by default. To customize HDR settings:

1. Touch the [icon] icon. The Settings screen appears.
2. Scroll down and touch **Photos + Camera**. The Photos and Camera Settings screen appears.
3. Touch the [ON] switch next to 'Keep Normal Photo'. The [OFF] switch appears and the iPhone will now delete non-HDR photos while keeping the HDR copy.
4. Touch the [OFF] switch next to 'Keep Normal Photo'. The [ON] switch appears and the iPhone will keep the non-HDR photo in addition to the HDR copy when taking photos.

Note: An HDR photo takes up more memory than a non-HDR one.

4. Customizing Video Playback Settings

After a video is stopped (not paused), the iPhone can resume playing it from the beginning or from where you last left off. To customize Video Playback settings:

1. Touch the icon. The Settings screen appears.
2. Scroll down and touch **Video**. The Video Settings screen appears, as shown in **Figure 3**.
3. Touch **Start Playing**. The Start Playing screen appears, as shown in **Figure 4**.
4. Touch **From Beginning**. A check mark appears next to the option and videos will now resume from the beginning.
5. Touch **Where Left Off**. A check mark appears next to the option and videos will now resume from where they last left off.

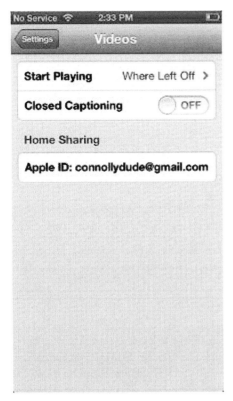

Figure 3: Video Settings Screen

5. Turning Closed Captioning On or Off

Closed Captioning is a feature that displays subtitles while playing videos that support it. To turn Closed Captioning on or off:

1. Touch the ![icon] icon. The Settings screen appears.
2. Scroll down and touch **Video**. The Video Settings screen appears.
3. Touch the OFF switch next to 'Closed Captioning'. The ON switch appears and Closed Captioning is turned on.
4. Touch the ON switch next to 'Closed Captioning'. The OFF switch appears and Closed Captioning is turned off.

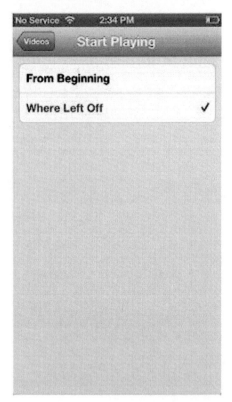

Figure 4: Start Playing Screen

Tips and Tricks

Table of Contents

1. Maximizing Battery Life

There are several things you can do to increase the battery life of the iPhone:

- Turn off the iPhone while it is charging. To do this, plug the iPhone in and then turn it off. Lock the iPhone whenever you are not using it. To lock the iPhone, press the **Sleep/Wake** button at the top of the phone. Refer to *"Button Layout"* on page 11 for the location of the Sleep/Wake button.
- Keep the Auto-lock feature on and set it to a small amount of time to wait before locking the phone when it is idle. Refer to *"Changing Auto-Lock Settings"* on page 233 to learn how to change Auto-lock settings.
- Turn down the brightness and turn off Auto-Brightness. Refer to *"Adjusting the Brightness"* on page 237 to learn how.
- Turn on Airplane mode in areas where there is little or no signal, as the iPhone will continually try to search for service. Refer to *"Turning Airplane Mode On or Off"* on page 206 to learn how to turn on Airplane Mode.
- Turn off 'Push' and manually fetch email when using the Mail application. Refer to *"Changing How You Receive Email"* on page 176 to learn how to change Mail settings.
- Make sure to let the battery drain completely and then charge it fully at least once a month. This will help both short-term and long-term battery life.
- Turn off Wi-Fi when it is not in use. Refer to *"Using Wi-Fi"* on page 29 to learn how. Turn off Location Services when they are not in use. Refer to *"Turning Location Services On or Off"* on page 207 to learn how.

2. Taking a Screenshot

To capture what is on the screen and save it as a photo, press and hold the **Home** button and then press the **Sleep/Wake** Button. Release the buttons and the screen will momentarily flash white. The screenshot is saved to the Camera Roll album.

3. Scrolling to the Top of a Screen

Touch anywhere in the bar at the very top of the screen to quickly scroll to the top of a list, website, etc. The bar is where the signal bars and battery meter are located.

4. Saving an Image While Browsing the Internet

To save an image from Safari to the iPhone, touch and hold the picture until the Image menu appears. Touch **Save Image**. The image is saved to the Camera Roll album.

5. Inserting a Period

When typing a sentence, touch the space bar twice quickly to insert a period and a space at the end of it.

6. Adding an Extension to a Contact's Number

When entering a number for a stored contact, you can add an extension that will be dialed

following a short pause after the call is connected. While entering a number, touch the button in the lower left-hand corner of the screen and then touch **Pause**. A comma appears and you can now type an extension. Each comma represents one second that the phone will wait.

7. Navigating the Home Screens

Typically, you get to another Home screen by touching the screen and sliding your finger to the left or right. Alternately, touch the bottom left or right corner of the screen for the same effect. In addition, you can touch one of the four gray dots at the bottom of a Home screen to go to the corresponding one.

8. Typing Alternate Characters

When typing a sentence, insert other characters, such as Á or Ñ, by touching and holding the base letter. A menu of characters appears above the letter. Touch a character to insert it.

9. Deleting Recently Typed Text

This feature is quite a secret. If you have just typed several lines of text and do not want any of it, just give the phone a good shake. A menu appears asking whether to undo the typing. Touch **Undo**. The typed text is erased. Give the phone another shake to redo the typing. This works in any application or while text messaging.

10. Resetting the iPhone

If the iPhone or an application freezes up or is acting strangely, you may wish to reset the iPhone. This will NOT wipe any data, but simply restart the operating system. To reset the iPhone, hold the **Home** button and **Sleep/Wake** button together until the phone completely shuts off. Continue to

hold the buttons until the logo appears. The phone resets and starts up.

11. Viewing the Full Horizontal Keyboard

The full horizontal keyboard provides much better accuracy than the vertical keyboard. Rotate the phone on either side while typing a text message or entering text in another application that supports it to turn on the horizontal keyboard.

12. Calling a Phone Number on a Website

You can call a phone number on a website directly. The number will be blue and underlined, much like a link. Touch the number. The iPhone calls it. If the number is on a website, the iPhone will ask whether to call the number. Touch **Call**. This may not work with all websites.

14. Taking Notes

A convenient way to take notes is by using the built-in Notes application and emailing the notes to yourself. To take notes, touch the   icon. Touch the   button at the top right of the screen to add a note. Touch the   icon at the bottom of the screen and then touch **Email** to email the note.

15. Recovering Signal After Being in an Area with No Service

Sometimes the iPhone has trouble finding signal after returning from an area where AT&T or Verizon was not available. This issue can sometimes be fixed by turning Airplane Mode on and then back off. Refer to *"Turning Airplane Mode On or Off"* on page 206 to learn how.

16. Changing the Number of Rings Before the iPhone Goes to Voicemail

There is a hidden way to change the number of times the iPhone rings before going to Voicemail. The maximum number of seconds the phone can ring is 30. Have a pen and paper ready, as you will need to enter a long number. To change the number of times the iPhone rings before going to Voicemail:

1. Touch the [phone icon] icon and then touch the [keypad icon] icon. The Keypad appears
2. Dial ***#61#** exactly as it appears here and touch the [Call] button. When the call is completed, the Voicemail Configuration screen appears, as shown in **Figure 1**.
3. Write down the number that follows "Forwards to." Skip the '+' since you will be typing it in later anyway.
4. Touch **Dismiss**. The call is ended.
5. Dial ***61*+1XXXXXXXXXX*11*tt#** exactly as it appears here, where the X's represent the number you just wrote down and "tt" is the number of seconds you want for the iPhone to ring before going to Voicemail. For example, if the number you wrote down is 1234567890 and the number of seconds you prefer is 30, you would dial *61*+11234567890*11*30#. To make the plus sign appear when dialing a phone number, touch and hold **0**.
6. Touch the [Call] button. The number of seconds the iPhone rings is changed and a confirmation appears, as shown in **Figure 2**.
7. Touch **Dismiss**. The call is ended.

Note: To change the ring time back, just repeat these steps. The number you wrote down in step three does not change, so you can proceed to step four if you know it. The default ring time for the iPhone is 20 seconds.

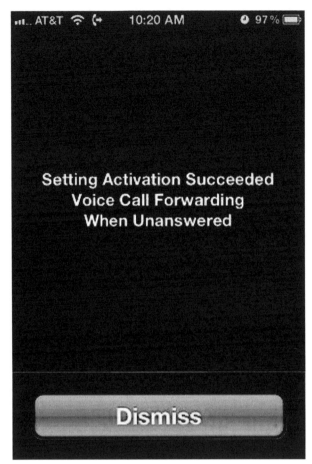

Figure 1: Voicemail Configuration Screen

Figure 2: Ring Time Changed Successfully

17. Changing the Navigation Icons in the iPod Application

You can change the arrangement of the Navigation icons in the iPod application. While using the iPod Application, touch the ▪▪▪ icon. The More screen appears. Touch **Edit** at the top right of the screen and then touch any icon on the page and drag it to the bottom of the screen. Release it over another icon. The icons are swapped.

18. Returning to the Last Screen in the Music Application

While listening to music, swipe the screen to the right instead of pressing the Back button to return to the last screen (songs, artists, etc.)

19. Deleting a Song in the Music Application

To delete a song from your iPhone, touch the song and swipe your finger to the left. The **Delete** button appears. Touch the **Delete** button. The song is deleted.

20. Taking a Picture from the Lock Screen

To take a picture without unlocking the phone, quickly press the **Home** button twice, and then touch the [camera] button. The camera turns on. Press the **Volume Up** button. The camera takes a picture.

21. Assigning a Custom Ringtone to a Contact

You can assign a custom ringtone to any contact in the Phonebook. To assign a ringtone to a contact:

1. Touch the icon. The Phonebook appears.
2. Find and touch the contact to whom you wish to assign a custom ringtone. The Contact Info screen appears. Refer to *"Finding a Contact"* on page 52 to learn how.
3. Touch **Edit** in the upper right-hand corner of the screen. The Contact Editing screen appears.
4. Touch **Ringtone**. A list of available ringtones appears.
5. Touch a ringtone. The ringtone plays.
6. Touch the **Save** button at the top right of the screen. The ringtone is selected and the Contact Editing screen appears.
7. Touch the **Done** button at the top right of the screen. The ringtone is assigned to the contact.

Note: Refer to "Buying Tones in iTunes" *on page 138 to learn how to purchase additional ringtones.*

22. Opening the Photos Application without Closing the Camera

To open the Photos application while the camera is turned on, touch the screen and slide your finger to the right. Touch the screen and move your finger to the left to return to the camera.

23. Inserting Emoticons

The Emoji keyboard contains over 460 new emoticons that can be used when entering text. To learn how to add the Emoji keyboard, refer to *"Adding an International Keyboard"* on page 224

and touch Emoji in step 6. After adding the Emoji keyboard, touch the key at the bottom of the virtual keyboard to switch to the Emoji keyboard while typing. The Emoji keyboard appears, as shown in **Figure 3**.

Figure 3: Emoji Keyboard

24. Hiding the Keyboard in the Messages

While reading a text message, you can hide the keyboard to view more of the conversation at once. Touch the last visible message in the conversation and slide your finger down to the keyboard. The keyboard is hidden.

Troubleshooting

Table of Contents

1. iPhone does not turn on

If the iPhone does not power on, try one or more of the following tips:
- **Recharge the iPhone** - Use the included wall charger to charge the battery. If the battery power is extremely low, the screen will not turn on for several minutes. Do NOT use the USB port on your computer to charge the iPhone.
- **Replace the battery** - If you purchased the iPhone a long time ago and have charged and discharged the battery 300-400 times, you may need to replace it. In this case, however, the iPhone may still turn on, but the battery will die much faster than it would in a newer iPhone. Contact Apple to learn how to replace your battery.
- **Reset the iPhone** – This method will not erase any data. Hold down the **Home** button and **Sleep/Wake** button at the same time for 10 seconds. Keep holding the two buttons until the

 logo appears and the phone restarts.

2. iPhone is not responding

If the iPhone is frozen or is not responding, try one or more of the following. These steps solve most problems on the iPhone.

- **Exit the Application** - If the phone freezes while running an application, hold the **Home** Button for six seconds. The application quits and the iPhone returns to the Home screen.
- **Turn the iPhone Off and then Back On** - If the iPhone is still frozen, try pressing the **Sleep/Wake** button to turn the iPhone off. Keep holding the Sleep/Wake Button until "Slide to Power Off" appears. Slide your finger from left to right over the text. The iPhone turns off. After the screen is completely black, press the **Sleep/Wake** button again to turn the phone back on.
- **Restart the iPhone** - Hold the **Home** button and **Sleep/Wake** button at the same time for 10 seconds or until the logo appears.
- **Remove Media** - Some downloaded applications or music may freeze up the iPhone. Try deleting some of the media that may be problematic after restarting the phone. Refer to *"Deleting an Application"* on page 198 to learn how to delete an application. You may also erase all data at once by doing the following:

Warning: Once erased, data cannot be recovered. Make sure you back up any files you wish to keep.

1. Touch the icon. The Settings screen appears.
2. Touch **General**. The General Settings screen appears.
3. Touch **Reset**. The Reset screen appears.
4. Touch **Erase All Content and Settings**. A confirmation appears.

3. Can't make a call

If the iPhone cannot make outgoing calls, try one of the following:

- If "No Service" is shown at the top left of the screen, the network does not cover you in your location. Try moving to a different location, or even to a different part of a building. Try walking around to find a better signal.
- Turn off Airplane Mode if you have it turned on. If that does not work, try turning Airplane Mode on for 15 seconds and then turning it off. Refer to *"Turning Airplane Mode On or Off"* on page 206 to learn how.
- Make sure you dialed 1 and an area code with the phone number.
- Turn the iPhone off and back on.

4. Signal Decreases when Covering Up Left Side of the Phone

There is a well-known issue with the iPhone, which causes it to lose signal dramatically when covering up the black gap in the metal on the left side of the phone. Some refer to this as the "death grip." While some suggestions include, "don't hold it like that" or "hold it with your right hand", there is no real fix for this problem. Apple used to issue rubber bumpers for free, but you will now need to purchase one. The bumper completely eliminates the problem. Using a case for the phone also fixes this issue, as it eliminates contact between your skin and the gap. Some people have also found that simply covering the gap with a piece of duct tape helps.

5. Can't surf the web

If you have no internet access, there may be little or no service in your area. Try moving to a different location or turning on Wi-Fi. To learn how to turn on Wi-Fi, refer to *"Using Wi-Fi"* on page 29. If you still can't get online, refer to *"iPhone is not responding"* on page 297 for further assistance.

6. Screen or keyboard does not rotate

If the screen does not rotate or the full, horizontal keyboard is not showing when you rotate the phone, it may be one of these issues:
- The application does not support the horizontal view.
- The iPhone is lying flat. Hold the iPhone upright to change the view in applications that support it.
- The rotation lock is on. Press the **Home** button twice quickly and scroll all the way to the left to check. Touch the icon. Screen rotation is unlocked.

7. iTunes does not detect iPhone

If iTunes does not detect the iPhone when connecting it to your computer, try using a different USB port. If that does not work, turn the iPhone off and on again while it is plugged in to the computer. If the iPhone indicates that it is connected, the problem might be with your computer. Try restarting your computer or reinstalling iTunes. Otherwise, refer to *"iPhone is not responding"* on page 296 for assistance.

8. iPhone does not ring or play music, can't hear while talking, can't listen to voicemails

Make sure the volume is turned up. Refer to *"Button Layout"* on page 11 to find the Volume Controls. Check whether you can still hear sound through headphones. The headphone jack is located on the top of the iPhone. If you can hear sound through headphones, try inserting the headphones and taking them out several times. Sometimes the sensor in the headphone jack malfunctions.

9. Low Microphone Volume, Caller can't hear you

If you are talking to someone who can't hear you, try the following:

- Take off any cases or other accessories as these may cover up the microphone.
- When you first take the iPhone out of the box, it comes with a piece of plastic covering the microphone. Make sure to take this plastic off before using the iPhone.
- If the caller cannot hear you at all, you may have accidentally muted the conversation. Refer to *"Using the Mute Function During a Voice Call"* on page 44 to learn how turn Mute on or off.

10. Camera does not work

If the iPhone camera is not functioning correctly, try one of the following:
- Clean the camera lens with a polishing cloth.
- Take off any cases or accessories that may interfere with the camera lens on the back of the iPhone.
- Hold the phone steady when taking a picture. A shaky hand often results in a blurry picture.
- Try leaning against a stationary object to stabilize your hand.

- If you cannot find the icon on your Home screen, try the following:

    1. Touch the icon. The Settings screen appears.
    2. Touch **General**. The General Settings screen appears.
    3. Touch **Restrictions**. The Restrictions screen appears.
    4. Touch **Disable Restrictions**. All restrictions are disabled.

11. iPhone shows the White Screen of Death

If the iPhone screen has gone completely white, try restarting or restoring the phone. Refer to *"iPhone is not responding"* on page 297 to learn how.

12. "iPhone needs to cool down" message appears

If you leave the iPhone in your car on a hot day or expose it to direct sunlight for too long, one of the following may happen:

- Device stops charging
- Weak signal Screen dims
- iPhone breaks completely
- "iPhone needs to cool down" message appears

Before using the iPhone, allow it to cool. The iPhone works best in temperatures between 32°F and 95°F (0°C to 35°C). While it is turned off, store the iPhone at temperatures between -4°F and 113°F (-20°C to 45°C).

13. Display does not adjust brightness automatically

If the iPhone does not brighten in bright conditions or does not become dimmer in dark conditions, try taking any cases or accessories off. A case may block the light sensor, located at the top of the phone near the earpiece. Also, check to make sure that Auto-Brightness is turned on. Refer to *"Adjusting the Brightness"* on page 237 to learn how to turn on Auto-Brightness.

Index

Printed in Great Britain
by Amazon